TOEFL®iBT

Vocabulary
PowerBuilder
Flashcards

Taiwan Edition

Lucia Hu
Doctor of Education
Applied Linguistics
Columbia University
New York, NY

Research & Education Association
Visit our website at
www.rea.com

For all references in this book, TOEFL® is a registered trademark of Educational Testing Service (ETS) and Test of English as a Foreign Language™ is a trademark of ETS.

Research & Education Association
61 Ethel Road West
Piscataway, New Jersey 08854
E-mail: info@rea.com

TOEFL® iBT
Vocabulary PowerBuilder Flashcards

Taiwan Edition

Printed in the United States of America

Library of Congress Control Number 2007932693

ISBN-13: 978-0-7386-0311-7
ISBN-10: 0-7386-0311-2

From the Author

We chose the vocabulary for this book from two major sources: (1) words that have appeared on actual TOEFL tests, and (2) words that are frequently used in academic settings. Learning these words will help you on the TOEFL and in college.

We seek to build upon what Taiwanese high school students already know. You will probably notice that in the example sentences that introduce you to new vocabulary items, many of the words are from lists provided by the College Entrance Center of Taiwan.

Further, you will notice that we provide the basic uninflected form of a word in our vocabulary list. Nouns are in the singular, and verbs are in the infinitival form. Of course, when the vocabulary words are used in sentences, they are inflected and can play different grammatical roles. Comparing the basic dictionary form with what you find in the sentence should help to learn meanings and usage.

You will encounter vocabulary questions in the reading section of the TOEFL iBT, and, of course, the size and quality of your English lexicon can have a substantial impact on your performance on other areas of the test. A TOEFL vocabulary question asks the test taker to identify the meaning of a word in the context in which it occurs. To give an easy example, *John drank a **can** of soda* and *Sally **can** speak Chinese* are two very different contexts where the three letters c-a-n indicate two different words, meanings, and parts of speech. A word may have several meanings and synonyms, but there are usually only a very small number of words that can be used interchangeably in a given context. Sometimes, a word cannot be replaced by another word without the sentence losing its original meaning.

In light of the realities of the TOEFL and of learning vocabulary, the meanings/synonyms provided for the words in this book are context-based. Wherever possible, the word meanings that we give are words that students learn in high school. The Chinese definitions that we provide should help readers get a better grasp of the nuances of the new words they are learning.

A distinctive and helpful feature of this book is that we group words according to how the TOEFL iBT categorizes its questions. Words are organized into five areas: (1) Arts, (2) Life Science, (3) Physical Science, (4) Social Science, and (5) College Life.

There is a further advantage to this book. Although the TOEFL test does not assume a test taker to have any prior knowledge of the subject materials on the exam, our readers will gain familiarity with the topics that frequently appear on the test since we write about the topics that appear frequently on the TOEFL.

We cluster sentences together by topic. This should enable you to learn vocabulary more systematically and help you gain confidence in reading passages of several sentences.

We hope that this book helps you to do well on TOEFL and master the English language. Thank you for giving us the opportunity to help you.

Good luck!

Lucia Hu, Ed.D.
Applied Linguistics
Columbia University

Author Acknowledgments

The author would like to thank Rachel Hu for assisting in re-searching and compiling the corpus; Mei-hua Chen for her valuable suggestions and professional insights that greatly helped to shape the book; Michael Mnentro, whose reading of the manuscript and intel-lectual discussions of language were indispensable to the completion of this book.

Master TOEFL Test Vocabulary – in a Flash!

If you picked up this flashcard book, you want to build your word power.

Our 1,000-plus vocabulary words were carefully chosen by an expert in word usage to give you a special advantage as you prepare for the Internet-based TOEFL test. One thousand words may seem like a lot, but consider that the TOEFL test's content is created from a database of 2.7 million words!

Our flashcard book is a unique toolkit for building vocabulary mastery, yet we designed it to be familiar and easy to use. We employ Kenyon & Knott phonetic symbols to indicate pronunciations. For Chinese speakers, each entry is shown using traditional Chinese characters.

The flip side of each card features a definition and college-level sentence.

We present the words in the same general topic categories as the test:

- Arts
- Life Science
- Physical Science
- Social Science
- College Life

This context will also help you master the small things about English that can make such a big difference when you're learning the language.

We carefully crafted this book in a way that will help you on the TOEFL test--and beyond it as well! Mastering this vocabulary is an investment in your future success.

Good luck on the TOEFL test, and best wishes in your educational pursuits!

Larry B. Kling
Chief Editor

About Research & Education Association

Founded in 1959, Research & Education Association (REA) is dedicated to publishing the finest and most effective educational materials–including software, study guides, and test preps–for students in middle school, high school, college, graduate school, and beyond.

REA's test preparation series includes books and software for all academic levels in almost all disciplines. REA publishes test preps for students who have not yet entered high school, as well as high school students preparing to enter college. Students at every level, in every field, with every ambition can find what they are looking for among REA's publications.

REA's series presents tests that accurately depict the official exams in both degree of difficulty and types of questions. REA's publications and educational materials are highly regarded and continually receive an unprecedented amount of praise from professionals, instructors, librarians, parents, and students. Our authors are as diverse as the subject matter represented in the books we publish. They are well known in their respective disciplines and serve on the faculties of prestigious colleges and universities throughout the United States and Canada.

Today REA's wide-ranging catalog is a leading resource for teachers, students, and professionals.

We invite you to visit us at *www.rea.com* to find out how "REA is making the world smarter."

Acknowledgments

We would like to thank Larry B. Kling, Vice President, Editorial, for his overall direction; Pam Weston, Vice President, Publishing, for setting the quality standards for production integrity and managing the publication to completion; Allice Leonard, Senior Editor, for project management and preflight editorial review; Jeff Lobalbo, Senior Graphic Artist, for font management and post-production file mapping; Christine Saul, Senior Graphic Designer, for designing our cover; Kathy Caratozzolo of Caragraphics for typesetting the manuscript and creating the index, and Wendell Anderson of North Star Writing & Editing for copyediting.

Table of Contents

Section I:
Arts ....Pages 1 to 114

Section II:
Life Science...Pages 115 to 242

Section III:
Physical Science..Pages 243 to 374

Section IV:
Social Science ....Pages 375 to 616

Section V:
College Life...Pages 617 to 672

Index ....Pages 671 to 680

Questions

Q–1

ARBITRARY
[`arbəˌtrɛrɪ] : 主觀的

Your Answer _____

_____

Q–2

ENTHRALL
[ɪn`θrɔl] : 著迷

Your Answer _____

_____

Q–3

BUCOLIC
[bju`kɑlɪk] : 鄉村的

Your Answer _____

_____

Correct Answers

A–1

a.—subjective

It seems **arbitrary** to say what art is.

A–2

v.—fascinate

Some people do not care much about art, while others are **enthralled** by it.

A–3

a.—rural

American painter Winslow Homer went out into the countryside and made himself famous by painting quiet scenes of **bucolic** life.

Questions

Q–4

ILLUMINATE
[ɪˋlumə‚net] : 闡明

Your Answer _____

Q–5

ENDOWMENT
[ɪnˋdaʊmənt] : 捐贈的基金

Your Answer _____

Q–6

EXTENSIVE
[ɪkˋstɛnsɪv] : 廣泛的

Your Answer _____

Correct Answers

A–4

v.—highlight
Some artists faithfully paint scenes from nature and avoid hidden messages; others might use their art to **illuminate** social or political issues.

A–5

n.—fund, gift
Museums often campaign to increase their **endowments**.

A–6

a.—wide
The Metropolitan Museum of Art has an **extensive** collection that spans thousands of years.

Questions

Q–7

ELUCIDATE
[ɪˋlusə͵det] : 解説

Your Answer

Q–8

GRUMBLE
[ˋgrʌmbl̩] : 嘀咕發牢騷

Your Answer

Q–9

FIGMENT
[ˋfɪgmənt] : 幻想

Your Answer

Correct Answers

A–7

v.—explain

If you take a tour of the Metropolitan Museum of Art, knowledgeable guides will help **elucidate** the artistic and historical background behind the exhibits.

A–8

v.—complain

Patrons at the Metropolitan Museum of Art **grumbled** when some paintings were put into glass cases to protect them.

A–9

n.—fantasy

Some of the paintings of Salvador Dali look like **figments** of the imagination.

Questions

Q–10

SMEAR
[smɪr] : 塗抹

Your Answer _____

_____

Q–11

APPRAISAL
[əˋprezḷ] : 評估，估價

Your Answer _____

_____

Q–12

AVARICE
[ˋævərɪs] : 貪婪

Your Answer _____

_____

Correct Answers

A–10

v.—spread

Many artists **smear** paint onto canvas with a small knife, not a paintbrush.

A–11

n.—estimate, evaluation, valuation

It is a good idea to get an **appraisal** before you buy or sell a piece of artwork.

A–12

n.—greed

The **avarice** of collectors sometimes causes them to purchase stolen art.

Questions

Q–13

COUNTERFEIT
[ˈkaʊntəˌfɪt] : 仿冒品

Your Answer _____

Q–14

CONSORT
[kənˈsɔrt] : 合夥

Your Answer _____

Q–15

IRATE
[aɪˈret] : 生氣的

Your Answer _____

Correct Answers

A–13

n.—imitation

A professional collector is able to tell a **counterfeit** from an authentic work.

A–14

v.—associate

The collector who **consorts** with art thieves is likely to get into trouble.

A–15

a.—angry

Museumgoers in Europe were **irate** when *The Scream*, a famous painting by Edvard Munch, was stolen.

Questions

Arts

Q–16

LUSTROUS
[ˋlʌstrəs] : 有光澤的

Your Answer

Q–17

NOCTURNAL
[nɑkˋtɚnḷ] : 夜晚的

Your Answer

Q–18

FRAYED
[fred] : 磨損的

Your Answer

11

Correct Answers

A–16

a.—shining

Some Japanese screen paintings have a **lustrous** golden background.

A–17

a.—nighttime, nightly

One of Rembrandt's best loved paintings is the **nocturnal** scene of *The Night Watch*.

A–18

a.—ragged

A frame can make a painting look nicer, and it can also keep the edges of the canvas from getting **frayed**.

Questions

Q–19

TREACHEROUS
[`trɛtʃərəs] : 不忠的

Your Answer _____

_____

Q–20

PLUNDER
[`plʌndɚ] : 劫奪

Your Answer _____

_____

Q–21

CRASS
[kræs] : 拙劣的

Your Answer _____

_____

Correct Answers

A–19

a.—dishonest

Hermann Goering proved to be a **treacherous** friend to the world of art because he stole famous paintings from many museums.

A–20

v.—steal

Some of the artwork that Goering **plundered** was eventually returned to its rightful owners.

A–21

a.—crude

What might seem beautiful and luxurious to one generation might be **crass** bad taste to the next.

Questions

Q–22

AESTHETIC
[εs`θεtιk] : 審美觀

Your Answer _____

Q–23

COVE
[kov] : 小海灣

Your Answer _____

Q–24

TYRO
[`taιro] : 新手，初學者

Your Answer _____

Correct Answers

A–22

n.—artistic system

Although most of us look at a painting for the image it conveys, students of art realize that there is a whole complex **aesthetic** to such details as the kinds of paint and canvas that the artist uses.

A–23

n.—small bay

Amateur painters often enjoy painting a forest or a quiet **cove**.

A–24

n.—beginner

It is virtually impossible for a **tyro** to produce a great painting.

Questions

Q–25

PIGMENT
[`pɪgmənt] : 顏料

Your Answer

Q–26

OPAQUE
[o`pek] : 不透明的

Your Answer

Q–27

TRANSLUCENT
[træns`lusn̩t] : 有透光性，半透明的

Your Answer

Correct Answers

A–25

n.—color
Different paints can be classified according to what kind of material is mixed with **pigments**.
Tempera paint is a combination of **pigment** and egg yolk; oil paint is a mix of **pigment** and oil.

A–26

a.—nontransparent
Some pigments are **opaque**, and light cannot pass through them.

A–27

a.—semitransparent
Pigments become **translucent** when they are mixed with oil. The **translucent** quality gives the paint an appearance of light coming through. It is between opaque and transparent.

Questions

Q–28

IMPERVIOUS
[ɪmˋpɝvɪəs] : 能防滲的

Your Answer _____

Q–29

VARNISH
[ˋvɑrnɪʃ] : 透明亮光漆

Your Answer _____

Q–30

SECRETE
[sɪˋkrit] : 分泌

Your Answer _____

Correct Answers

A–28

a.—resistant
Acrylic paint dries fast and is **impervious** to water.

A–29

n.—glossy transparent coating, coat
Clear **varnish** can protect a painting and keep its colors fresh for a long time.

A–30

v.—produce
Some varnishes are from trees, and some are from insects that **secrete** sticky, shining substances.

Questions

Q–31

IRREPARABLE
[ɪˋrɛpərəbḷ] : 無法修補的

Your Answer ⎯⎯⎯⎯⎯⎯⎯⎯⎯⎯⎯⎯⎯⎯⎯⎯⎯⎯⎯⎯⎯

⎯⎯⎯⎯⎯⎯⎯⎯⎯⎯⎯⎯⎯⎯⎯⎯⎯⎯⎯⎯⎯⎯⎯⎯⎯⎯⎯

Q–32

SPONTANEOUS
[spɑnˋtenɪəs] : 自然的

Your Answer ⎯⎯⎯⎯⎯⎯⎯⎯⎯⎯⎯⎯⎯⎯⎯⎯⎯⎯⎯⎯

⎯⎯⎯⎯⎯⎯⎯⎯⎯⎯⎯⎯⎯⎯⎯⎯⎯⎯⎯⎯⎯⎯⎯⎯⎯⎯⎯

Q–33

EXPONENT
[ɪkˋsponənt] : 代表者

Your Answer ⎯⎯⎯⎯⎯⎯⎯⎯⎯⎯⎯⎯⎯⎯⎯⎯⎯⎯⎯⎯

⎯⎯⎯⎯⎯⎯⎯⎯⎯⎯⎯⎯⎯⎯⎯⎯⎯⎯⎯⎯⎯⎯⎯⎯⎯⎯⎯

Correct Answers

A–31

a.—cannot be repaired

Many artists choose not to varnish acrylic paintings because **irreparable** damage often occurs in the process.

A–32

a.—natural, unplanned

Action painting reveals the artist's **spontaneous** creativity through the drips and splashes left on the canvas.

A–33

n.—representative

Jackson Pollock, an American painter, was the leading **exponent** of action painting.

Questions

Q–34

TRICKLE
[`trɪk!] : 慢慢地流

Your Answer _____

Q–35

TAUT
[tɔt] : 拉緊的

Your Answer _____

Q–36

OBSOLETE
[ˌɑbsə`lit][`ɑbsəˌlit] : 廢棄不用的

Your Answer _____

Correct Answers

A–34

v.—drip

Pollock was reported to dance on the canvases that were laid on the floor as he painted, and he would let paint **trickle** on them.

A–35

a.—tight

Canvas should be **taut** and without wrinkles before you paint on it.

A–36

a.—outdated

Some people say that realistic painting became **obsolete** when photography was invented.

Questions

GENUINE
[ˋdʒɛnjʊɪn]：真實的

Your Answer

ESCHEW
[ɛˋʃu][ɛsˋtʃu]：避免

Your Answer

SHACKLE
[ˋʃækl̩]：束縛

Your Answer

Correct Answers

A–37

a.—real

Although painting is still an important form of art, its use in capturing **genuine** events and important people of the day was taken over by photography in the nineteenth century.

A–38

v.—avoid

Some professional photographers still **eschew** the use of digital cameras.

A–39

n.—bond, restraint

Books have helped people to break the **shackles** of ignorance.

Questions

Q–40

SMUDGE
[smʌdʒ] : 使模糊

Your Answer _____

Q–41

SCRUTINY
[`skrutn̩ɪ] : 詳細審視

Your Answer _____

Q–42

EMBELLISH
[ɪm`bɛlɪʃ] : 誇張渲染

Your Answer _____

Correct Answers

A–40

v.—blur

Before modern inks were invented, newsprint could easily be **smudged**.

A–41

n.—analysis

A newspaper article must be able to hold up under careful **scrutiny** and fact checking.

A–42

v.—exaggerate

A reporter must resist the temptation to **embellish** a story to make it sound better.

Questions

Q–43

COMPILE
[kəm`paɪl] : 累積

Your Answer _____

_____

Q–44

DISTORT
[dɪs`tɔrt]: 扭曲

Your Answer _____

_____

Q–45

PRESTIGE
[prɛs`tɪdʒ] : 名望

Your Answer _____

_____

Correct Answers

A–43

v.—accumulate

Some newspapers have **compiled** an impressive record of having reported important stories first.

A–44

v.—twist

Some publications **distort** the news for political reasons.

A–45

n.—reputation

Serious journalistic mistakes can damage a newspaper's **prestige**.

Questions

Q–46

FABRICATE
[`fæbrɪˌket] : 杜撰

Your Answer _____

_____

Q–47

FRAUDULENT
[`frɔdʒələnt] : 欺詐的

Your Answer _____

_____

Q–48

PROCRASTINATE
[proˋkræstəˌnet] : 拖延

Your Answer _____

_____

Correct Answers

A–46

v.—fake, make up

If a journalist **fabricates** a story, he could destroy his own career.

A–47

a.—dishonest

Reporters seek to uncover the **fraudulent** behavior of companies that deceive the public.

A–48

v.—delay

Reporters cannot **procrastinate** because they have deadlines almost every day.

Questions

Q–49

DIVERT
[də`vɜt] [daɪ`vɜt] : 轉移

Your Answer _____

_____

Q–50

BOLSTER
[`bolstə] : 加強

Your Answer _____

_____

Q–51

COMPLIMENTARY
[ˌkɑmplə`mɛntərɪ] : 免費贈送的

Your Answer _____

_____

Correct Answers

A–49

v.—redirect

Newspapers, even popular ones, are having difficulty keeping companies from **diverting** money to Web-based advertising.

A–50

v.—strengthen

To **bolster** readership, some companies give their magazines away.

A–51

a.—free

Some magazine subscriptions are **complimentary**.

Questions

ANNOTATE
[ˋæno͵tet] : 作註解

Your Answer _____

_____

JUMBLE
[ˋdʒʌmbl̩] : 使混亂

Your Answer _____

_____

GAZETTE
[gəˋzɛt] : 報紙

Your Answer _____

_____

Correct Answers

A–52

v.—note, comment
Some people **annotate** the books they read with handwritten notes.

A–53

v.—mix
If you own only a few books, it is alright to **jumble** them together, but if you have a lot, they have to be organized in some way.

A–54

n.—newspaper
Many magazines and **gazettes** are now available on the World Wide Web.

Questions

Q–55

CURSORY
[`kɜsərɪ] : **匆匆的**

Your Answer

Q–56

PEJORATIVE
[pə`dʒɔrətɪv] : **負面的，輕蔑的**

Your Answer

Q–57

HYPERBOLIC
[haɪpə`bɑlɪk] : **誇張的**

Your Answer

Correct Answers

A–55

a.—hasty

Nowadays, few people have the time to read a newspaper cover to cover, so most readers give each page a **cursory** glance.

A–56

a.—negative

Yellow journalism is a **pejorative** term to refer to the news media or journalists who use sensationalized news to attract readers.

A–57

a.—exaggerated

Even though they believe in the social responsibilities of newspapers, some publishers try to gain success through **hyperbolic** stories.

Questions

Q–58

HEINOUS
[`henəs] : 殘忍的

Your Answer _____

Q–59

EXPURGATE
[`ɛkspɚˌget] : 刪除

Your Answer _____

Q–60

CONCEDE
[kən`sid] : 承認

Your Answer _____

Correct Answers

A–58

a.—cruel

Some media report **heinous** crimes in detail.

A–59

v.—remove

To maintain circulation, some publishers do not **expurgate** vulgar material from news stories.

A–60

v.—admit

Some publishers **concede** that the demands of business can affect the news.

Questions

Q–61

HAPHAZARD
[ˌhæp`hæzəd] : 未經規畫的，隨便的

Your Answer _____

_____

Q–62

DIVERSE
[də`vɜs][daɪ`vɜs] : 多種不同的

Your Answer _____

_____

Q–63

HECTIC
[`hɛktɪk] : 匆忙的

Your Answer _____

_____

Correct Answers

A–61

a.—unplanned

The layouts of some cities are carefully planned, but in others, the order of streets is **haphazard**.

A–62

a.—different

Cities in America are **diverse** and have people from many different countries.

A–63

a.—rapid

Some people love the **hectic** pace of cities like New York and Tokyo.

Questions

Q–64

TRANQUIL
[ˋtræŋkwɪl] : 平靜的

Your Answer _____

Q–65

SECLUDED
[sɪˋkludɪd] : 離群索居的

Your Answer _____

Q–66

OUTLYING
[ˋaʊtˌlaɪɪŋ] : 偏遠的

Your Answer _____

Correct Answers

A–64

a.—peaceful

In the 1950s, many Americans left big cities for a **tranquil** life in the suburbs.

A–65

a.—isolated

It used to be that if you wanted to live a **secluded** life, you had to have a house in the country.

A–66

a.—remote

In some nations, there are still no suburbs, and beyond the **outlying** districts of the cities, there is only farmland.

Questions

Q–67

UNSETTLING
[ʌn`sɛtlɪŋ] : 紛擾的，不安的

Your Answer _____

_____

Q–68

IMPROVISE
[`ɪmprəvaɪz] : 隨機應變

Your Answer _____

_____

Q–69

QUALM
[kwɑm] : 顧慮，不安

Your Answer _____

_____

Correct Answers

A–67

a.—upsetting

When a person from a small, quiet town visits a big, noisy city, the experience can be **unsettling**.

A–68

v.—to perform without previous preparation

To live successfully in a big city, you have to be able to **improvise** when there are problems with the subway.

A–69

n.—uneasiness

Some people have no **qualms** about lying and deceiving others.

Questions

Q–70

SCRUPLE
[`skrup!] : 道德良知

Your Answer _____

_____

Q–71

PETRIFY
[`pɛtrə͵faɪ`] : 石化

Your Answer _____

_____

Q–72

SUPERSEDE
[͵supɚ`sid] : 取代

Your Answer _____

_____

Correct Answers

A–70

n.—moral
Many nineteenth-century industrial leaders were men with few **scruples** who cared only about money.

A–71

v.—fossilize
Coal is dead plant material that is millions of years old and has become **petrified**.

A–72

v.—replace
The use of oil has **superseded** the use of coal in many cases.

Questions

Q–73

TRAVERSE
[trə`vɚs] [`trævɚs] : 橫越

Your Answer _____

_____

Q–74

EXTORT
[ɪk`stɔrt] : 敲詐

Your Answer _____

_____

Q–75

BIGOTRY
[`bɪgətrɪ] : 固執成見

Your Answer _____

_____

Correct Answers

A–73

v.—cross

Oil companies **traverse** the globe in search of new petroleum deposits.

A–74

v.—cheat

Some business owners look on union leaders as people trying to **extort** money from them.

A–75

n.—bias

Some people say that there is less **bigotry** in a big city than there is in a small town.

Questions

Q–76

INCENTIVE
[ɪn`sɛntɪv] : 動機

Your Answer _____

_____

Q–77

CHASM
[`kæzəm] : 懸殊，隔閡

Your Answer _____

_____

Q–78

RECOURSE
[`rikɔrs] [rɪ`kors] : 求助

Your Answer _____

_____

Correct Answers

A–76

n.—motive

Often, people are drawn to cities because they hope to make more money, but sometimes governments need to provide **incentives** to make people relocate to cities.

A–77

n.—gap

There seems to be a **chasm** between the rich and the poor in many cities.

A–78

n.—resort

Workers who feel wronged by their employer have **recourse** to their union or to the government.

Questions

Q–79

DISPLACE
[dɪsˋples] : 排擠掉，取代

Your Answer _____

Q–80

SNARL
[ˋsnɑrl] : 纏繞，混亂

Your Answer _____

Q–81

AVOW
[əˋvaʊ] : 聲明承諾

Your Answer _____

Correct Answers

A–79

v.—force out
Some people believe that immigrants **displace** native-born people from entry-level jobs.

A–80

v.—tangle
When traffic becomes badly **snarled** in a big city, drivers can sit motionless for hours.

A–81

v.—promise
More than one politician hoping to win the vote of the urban poor has **avowed** that he would "put a chicken in every pot."

Questions

Q–82

CURTAIL
[kəˋtel] : 減少

Your Answer _____

_____

Q–83

ASSIMILATE
[əˋsɪmḷˏet] : 同化

Your Answer _____

_____

Q–84

ENLIST
[ɪnˋlɪst] : 登記入伍

Your Answer _____

_____

Correct Answers

A–82

v.—decrease

When a city **curtails** spending on road repairs, you will see a lot of holes in the road a few months later.

A–83

v.—adjust

Many European immigrants **assimilated** to American culture in a generation.

A–84

v.—enroll

Many recent immigrants have **enlisted** in the army.

Questions

Q–85

SUSTAINABLE
[sə`stenəbḷ] : 可承擔負荷的

Your Answer _____

Q–86

ACCESSIBILITY
[æk͵sɛsə`bɪlətɪ] : 便利性

Your Answer _____

Q–87

PARAMETER
[pə`ræmətə] : 指標

Your Answer _____

Correct Answers

A–85

a.—supportable
Affordable housing, good transportation, and **sustainable** development are common topics of interest among those many urban institutions that offer studies of city planning.

A–86

n.—availability
In recent years, city planners have tried to improve **accessibility** to mass transit for disabled people.

A–87

n.—guideline
A planner should not copy **parameters** for development from another city because what works in one place might fail in another.

Questions

Q–88

INFRASTRUCTURE
[ˋɪnfrəˏstrʌktʃɚ] : 基礎建設，基層結構

Your Answer _____

Q–89

CONCEIVABLE
[kənˋsivəbḷ] : 可想像的

Your Answer _____

Q–90

COLOSSAL
[kəˋlɑsḷ] : 巨大的

Your Answer _____

Correct Answers

A–88

n.—foundation

A good city planner knows that **infrastructures** such as electricity, water and sewage are important.

A–89

a.—imaginable

The Great Pyramid in Egypt is the only one of the original Seven Wonders of the World remaining today. Building a structure of its size even with modern equipment is not easily **conceivable**.

A–90

a.—huge

Egypt's **colossal** statues and pyramids attract tourists from around the world.

Questions

Q–91

PERPENDICULAR
[ˌpɝpənˋdɪkjələ] : 垂直的

Your Answer _____

Q–92

DEFY
[dɪˋfaɪ] : 抗拒，挑戰

Your Answer _____

Q–93

SURMOUNT
[sɚˋmaʊnt] : 克服

Your Answer _____

Correct Answers

A–91

a.—vertical
The Leaning Tower of Pisa is not **perpendicular**.

A–92

v.—challenge
In 1994, the American Society of Civil Engineers chose the seven greatest civil engineering achievements of the twentieth century, projects that **defied** the idea that "it couldn't be done."

A–93

v.—overcome
The Seven Wonders of the Modern World all have something in common: they overcame technical difficulties that seemed impossible to **surmount**.

Questions

Q–94

INCREDULOUS
[ɪn`krɛdʒələs] : 不可思議的

Your Answer

Q–95

INGENIOUS
[ɪn`dʒinjəs] : 獨創的

Your Answer

Q–96

UNPRECEDENTED
[ʌn`prɛsə‚dɛntɪd] : 前所未有的

Your Answer

Correct Answers

A–94

a.—disbelieving

People were **incredulous** about plans to dig a canal in Panama.

A–95

a.—innovative

The Panama Canal was an **ingenious** engineering project that greatly speeded shipping.

A–96

a.—groundbreaking

The builders of the Panama Canal faced many obstacles, but their work turned out to be an **unprecedented** success.

Questions

Q–97

SUCCUMB
[sə`kʌm] : 死於

Your Answer _____

_____

Q–98

RELENTLESSLY
[rɪ`lɛntləslɪ] : 不屈不撓地

Your Answer _____

_____

Q–99

ADAMANT
[`ædəmənt] : 堅決的，不屈不撓的

Your Answer _____

_____

Correct Answers

A–97

v.—die

More than 25,000 people died during the building of the canal. About 20,000 of them **succumbed** to malaria or yellow fever.

A–98

adv.—untiringly

After Joseph Strauss got the idea of building a bridge at San Francisco's Golden Gate in 1919, he **relentlessly** promoted the project.

A–99

a.—unyielding

He was **adamant** about the project of building the Golden Gate Bridge.

Questions

Q–100

PLUNGE
[plʌndʒ] : 陷入

Your Answer _____

Q–101

SUBSIDIZE
[`sʌbsəˌdaɪz] : 資助

Your Answer _____

Q–102

EFFACE
[ɪˋfes] : 抹滅

Your Answer _____

Correct Answers

A–100

v.—fall, drop
America **plunged** into the Great Depression at the end of 1929.

A–101

v.—finance
As a result of the Great Depression, the government would not **subsidize** the project of building the bridge; Joseph Strauss had to raise the funds locally.

A–102

v.—erase
Some people were against the idea of building a bridge at the Golden Gate; they were afraid that a bridge would **efface** the beauty of the area.

Questions

Q–103

CONSTRAINT
[kən`strent] : 限制

Your Answer

Q–104

FEASIBLE
[`fizəbl̩] : 可實行的

Your Answer

Q–105

ASSENT
[ə`sɛnt] : 同意

Your Answer

Correct Answers

A–103

n.—restriction

Joseph Strauss overcame many **constraints** in building the bridge.

A–104

a.—workable

He had to explain to many different groups of people that the project was **feasible**.

A–105

n.—agreement

In 1932, Joseph Strauss sought **assent** from Amadeo Giannini, the owner of the Bank of America, to help finance the project.

Questions

Q–106

EXPOUND

[ɪk`spaʊnd] : 解説

Your Answer _____

_____

Q–107

CRUCIAL

[`kruʃəl] : 決定性的，重要的

Your Answer _____

_____

Q–108

ASCRIBE

[ə`skraɪb] : 歸因於

Your Answer _____

_____

Correct Answers

A–106
v.—explain
Strauss **expounded** to Giannini how the bridge would help the economy of San Francisco.

A–107
a.—vital
It was acknowledged that Giannini's help was **crucial**.

A–108
v.—credit
Some people **ascribed** the completion of the bridge to Giannini's financial support.

Questions

Q–109

INTRICATE
[`ɪntrəkɪt] : 複雜的

Your Answer

Q–110

ASSIDUOUSLY
[ə`sɪdʒʊəslɪ] : 勤勉地

Your Answer

Q–111

ANTICIPATE
[æn`tɪsə͵pet] : 預見，事先準備

Your Answer

Correct Answers

A–109

a.—complex

Intricate calculations were involved in designing the Golden Gate Bridge, and most of the work was done by a professor named Charles Ellis.

A–110

adv.—diligently

For months, Charles Ellis **assiduously** worked more than twelve hours a day on the calculations for the bridge, including suspension ropes, cables and floor beams.

A–111

v.—foresee

Charles Ellis tried to **anticipate** all the problems that the bridge might encounter when he designed it.

Questions

Q–112

WRETCHED
[`rɛtʃɪd] : 悲慘的

Your Answer _____

_____

Q–113

UNDULY
[ʌn`djulɪ] : 過度地

Your Answer _____

_____

Q–114

HUE
[hju] : 色彩

Your Answer _____

_____

Correct Answers

A–112

a.—miserable
The workers building the bridge put up with **wretched** conditions.

A–113

adv.—excessively
They endured the cold, **unduly** high winds, and thick fog, and some of them had to work under water.

A–114

n.—color
The color of the Golden Gate Bridge is international orange. It is a shade of orange with a reddish **hue**.

Questions

Q–115

LUDICROUS
[`ludɪkrəs] : 可笑的

Your Answer _____

_____

Q–116

APPEAL
[ə`pil] : 吸引力

Your Answer _____

_____

Q–117

FLAMBOYANT
[flæm`bɔɪənt] : 像火焰的，華麗的

Your Answer _____

_____

Correct Answers

A–115

a.—ridiculous

When Irving Morrow first proposed to paint the bridge international orange, some officials of the Bridge Board thought his idea was **ludicrous** and suggested gray paint instead.

A–116

n.—attraction

The art deco style of the Golden Gate Bridge gives it an artistic **appeal**.

A–117

a.— showy

The Chrysler Building, a **flamboyant** skyscraper in the art deco style, was the tallest building in the world for a few short months before the Empire State Building surpassed it.

Questions

Q–118

EMBODY
[ɪm`bɑdɪ] : 包含

Your Answer _____

_____

Q–119

CONJECTURE
[kən`dʒɛktʃə] : 猜測

Your Answer _____

_____

Q–120

INCORPORATE
[ɪn`kɔrpə͵ret] : 包含

Your Answer _____

_____

Correct Answers

A–118

v.—include
The design emphasized upward motion through vertical lines and it **embodied** what was then considered modern in a building.

A–119

v.—guess
Walter Chrysler **conjectured** that owning the world's tallest building would be good advertising for his automobile company.

A–120

v.—include
He asked his architect to **incorporate** the features of Chrysler cars into the look of the building.

Questions

Q–121

CULMINATION
[ˌkʌlmə`neʃən] : **實現，成就**

Your Answer _____

_____

Q–122

MONUMENTAL
[ˌmɑnjə`mɛntl̩] : **驚人的**

Your Answer _____

_____

Q–123

STREAMLINE
[`strim.laɪn] : **流線，流線型**

Your Answer _____

_____

Correct Answers

A–121

n.—fulfillment, completion
The Empire State Building was the **culmination** of the efforts of many skilled workers and architects.

A–122

a.—awe-inspiring
With **monumental** effort, the construction of the Empire State Building was completed in one year and 45 days.

A–123

n.—flowing line
The **streamline** style was a feature of art and design in the 1930s and '40s.

Questions

Q–124

HALLMARK
[`hɔl.mɑrk] : 特色

Your Answer

Q–125

OFFSHOOT
[`ɔf.ʃut] : 分支

Your Answer

Q–126

DENOTE
[dɪ`not] : 表示

Your Answer

Correct Answers

A–124

n.—feature

The streamline style was a **hallmark** of architecture during the 1930s and '40s.

A–125

n.—branch

Some consider the streamline style as an **offshoot** of the art deco design.

A–126

v.—indicate

Streamlines can **denote** speed and give a sense of motion.

Questions

Q–127

EVOKE
[ɪˋvok] : **使聯想**

Your Answer _____

Q–128

MUNDANE
[mʌnˋden] : **普通的，日常的**

Your Answer _____

Q–129

WITHSTAND
[wɪðˋstænd] : **承受**

Your Answer _____

Correct Answers

A–127

v.—suggest
Streamlined products **evoked** a spirit of beauty and elegance.

A–128

a.—common, ordinary
The streamline style was so popular that it was applied to **mundane** objects such as chairs and pencil sharpeners.

A–129

v.—endure
Canada's CN Tower is widely considered to be one of the world's tallest freestanding structures on land, and it is able to **withstand** wind gusts up to 260 miles per hour.

Questions

Q–130

ADVOCATE
[`ædvəˌket] : 提倡

Your Answer _____

Q–131

STRIVE
[straɪv] : 努力，致力於

Your Answer _____

Q–132

REFURBISH
[ri`fɝbɪʃ] : 刷新，裝修

Your Answer _____

Correct Answers

A–130

v.—promote

William Morris (1834-1896), known as an artist and craftsman, strongly **advocated** the view that a work of art must be useful. If something is not useful, it is not beautiful.

A–131

v.—aim

Nowadays architects **strive** for simplicity—a value that William Morris considered most important for art.

A–132

v.—restore

In much of the world today, beautiful old buildings are being **refurbished** instead of being destroyed.

Questions

Q–133

RENOVATE
[`rɛnəˌvet] : 整修，翻新

Your Answer ⎯⎯⎯⎯⎯⎯⎯⎯⎯⎯⎯⎯⎯⎯

Q–134

FACADE
[fə`sɑd] : 建築物的正面

Your Answer ⎯⎯⎯⎯⎯⎯⎯⎯⎯⎯⎯⎯⎯⎯

Q–135

CENTENNIAL
[sɛn`tɛnɪəl] : 百年的

Your Answer ⎯⎯⎯⎯⎯⎯⎯⎯⎯⎯⎯⎯⎯⎯

Correct Answers

A–133

v.—remodel

Sometimes it costs more to **renovate** an old house than to build a new one.

A–134

n.—front of a building

The New York Public Library on Fifth Avenue is an architectural landmark known for its white-marble **facade** and two stone lions sitting at the grand entrance.

A–135

a.—100 years

The governor of New York recently announced a plan to help to restore the facade, and the restoration is expected to be completed by the library's **centennial** celebration in 2011.

Questions

Q–136

PERTAIN
[pɚˋten] : 關於

Your Answer

Q–137

PEDESTAL
[ˋpɛdɪstl̩] : 基座，底座

Your Answer

Q–138

SALVAGE
[ˋsælvɪdʒ] : 搶救

Your Answer

Correct Answers

A–136

v.—relate

In 1986, there were a lot of news stories **pertaining** to the 100th birthday of the Statue of Liberty.

A–137

n.—base

Most people know that the statue was a gift from France to America, but few are aware that the **pedestal** the statue stands upon was made by Americans.

A–138

v.—rescue

There are people who are interested in buying old building materials. Some people **salvage** items from condemned or wrecked buildings because they love art, while others do it for profit.

Questions

Q–139

FLIMSY
[`flɪmzɪ] : 脆弱的

Your Answer _____

_____

Q–140

DUMBFOUND
[ˌdʌm`faʊnd] : 驚訝

Your Answer _____

_____

Q–141

EMBLEM
[`ɛmbləm] : 象徵

Your Answer _____

_____

Correct Answers

A–139

a.—weak

Wood is fine for building small houses, but it is too **flimsy** for tall city buildings, which must be made of steel and concrete.

A–140

v.—amaze

People who look up at the sky in a big city are often **dumbfounded** by how a skyscraper looks different as the light changes.

A–141

n.—symbol

Skyscrapers have been an **emblem** of strength and progress for the past century, and New York City has many famous skyscrapers.

Questions

Q–142

EMULATE
[ˋɛmjəˌlet]: 仿效競爭

Your Answer _____

Q–143

REPUDIATE
[rɪˋpjudɪˌet] : 唾棄

Your Answer _____

Q–144

GAUDY
[ˋgɔdɪ] : 俗麗的

Your Answer _____

Correct Answers

A–142

v.—imitate

For the past few decades, many of the world's cities have been **emulating** New York.

A–143

v.—spurn

Before the Second World War, a number of European nations seemed to **repudiate** skyscrapers, preferring more traditional buildings of a lower height.

A–144

a.—flashy

Certain old architectural styles look too rich, too complicated, and overdecorated to us today. Although these buildings might have cost a fortune to construct, they seem cheap and **gaudy** to us now.

Questions

Q–145

AMENITY
[ə`mɛnətɪ][ə`minətɪ] : 舒適的設施

Your Answer _____

Q–146

INCONGRUITY
[ˌɪnkɑŋ`gruətɪ] : 不平衡，不協調

Your Answer _____

Q–147

MOTIF
[mo`tif] : 主題，主要特色

Your Answer _____

Correct Answers

A–145

n.—comfort

In order to compete for tenants, most modern apartment buildings are furnished with **amenities** such as an elegant lobby, fitness rooms, a swimming pool, and 24-hour security.

A–146

n.—unevenness, imbalance, disproportion

The **incongruity** between brand new buildings and ones that are centuries old gives many cities character.

A–147

n.—theme

Many historical towns do not accept a building proposal that disagrees with their established architectural **motif**.

Questions

Q–148

SLANT
[slænt] : 傾斜

Your Answer _____

Q–149

IMPECCABLE
[ɪmˋpɛkəb!] : 完美無瑕的

Your Answer _____

Q–150

LAVISH
[ˋlævɪʃ] : 豐富的，過多的

Your Answer _____

Correct Answers

A–148

v.—tilt

In cold regions, the roofs of houses usually **slant** so that the snow falls off more easily.

A–149

a.—flawless

Luxury hotels offer **impeccable** service to attract guests who are willing to pay to be pampered.

A–150

a.—luxurious

To attract tourists, many hotels have **lavish** decorations.

Questions

Q–151

FESTOON
[fɛsˋtun] : 用花綵裝飾

Your Answer _____

Q–152

ICON
[ˋaɪkɑn] : 泰斗，象徵性的人物

Your Answer _____

Q–153

PSEUDONYM
[ˋsjudn͵ɪm] : 筆名

Your Answer _____

Correct Answers

A–151

v.—decorate

At Christmastime, many towns **festoon** their streetlights with wreaths and red ribbons.

A–152

n.—symbol

Mark Twain is an **icon** of American literature.

A–153

n.—pen name

Mark Twain is the **pseudonym** of Samuel Clemens.

Questions

RECOUNT
[rɪˋkaʊnt] : 敍述

Your Answer _____

SATIRE
[ˋsætaɪr] : 諷刺，揶揄

Your Answer _____

ARDENT
[ˋɑrdənt] : 熱心的

Your Answer _____

Correct Answers

A–154

v.—tell

Some of Twain's work **recounts** his own experiences in a fictionalized form.

A–155

n.—irony, ridicule

Mark Twain expressed his political and social views through humor and **satire**.

A–156

a.—enthusiastic

Twain was an **ardent** champion of human freedom.

Questions

Q–157

ZENITH
[ˋzinɪθ] : 頂點

Your Answer

Q–158

ALOOF
[əˋluf] : 遠離的

Your Answer

Q–159

RACONTEUR
[ˌrækɑnˋtɝ] : 擅於說故事的人

Your Answer

Correct Answers

A–157

n.—top, peak
Some people say that Mark Twain reached the **zenith** of his literary powers when he wrote Huckleberry Finn.

A–158

a.—distant
Some famous writers love to give talks and meet with people while others remain **aloof** from the public.

A–159

n.—storyteller
Mark Twain was a **raconteur** who loved to tell amusing tales.

Questions

Q–160

ENRAPTURE
[ɪnˋræptʃɚ] : 滿心歡喜

Your Answer _____

_____

Q–161

ALLUSION
[əˋluʒən] : 參考，引用

Your Answer _____

_____

Q–162

JARRING
[ˋdʒɑrɪŋ] : 刺耳不悅的

Your Answer _____

_____

Correct Answers

A–160

v.—delight
Many people are **enraptured** by hearing the music of Mozart played well.

A–161

n.—reference
Sometimes, one composer will make an **allusion** to another composer in a piece of music.

A–162

a.—unpleasant
In the early twentieth century, many concertgoers found listening to the music of Igor Stravinsky a **jarring** experience.

Questions

Q–163

JANGLE
[`dʒæŋgl̩] : 使難受刺耳

Your Answer _____

_____

Q–164

DISSONANCE
[`dɪsənəns] : 不和諧的音調

Your Answer _____

_____

Q–165

REMNANT
[`rɛmnənt] : 遺風，（風貌的）遺存

Your Answer _____

_____

Correct Answers

A–163

v.—rattle

Today's new music can **jangle** against the nerves of older listeners.

A–164

n.—disharmony

Classical composers such as Mozart avoided **dissonance**.

A–165

n.—remainder

An orchestra conductor dressing up in a white tie and tails is a **remnant** of nineteenth-century fashion.

Questions

Q–166

ACUMEN
[æ`k jəmən] : 聰明才智

Your Answer _____

Q–167

INTEGER
[`ɪntədʒə] : 整數

Your Answer _____

Q–168

DEXTEROUS
[`dɛkstərəs] : 靈巧的

Your Answer _____

Correct Answers

A–166

n.—intelligence, keenness
It takes considerable **acumen** to read music.

A–167

n.—whole number
When writing music numerically, one uses the
integers from 1 to 7.

A–168

a.—skillful
You have to be **dexterous** to play the piano well.

Questions

Q–169

TERMINOLOGY
[ˌtɝməˈnɑlədʒɪ] : 專門術語

Your Answer _____

_____

Q–170

TRANSITORY
[ˈtrænsəˌtorɪ] : 短暫的

Your Answer _____

_____

Q–171

SUPERFLUOUS
[sʊˈpɝfluəs] : 不必要的

Your Answer _____

_____

Correct Answers

A–169

n.—technical terms

In the **terminology** of music, tempo means "the speed of a piece."

A–170

a.—temporary

The ancient Greek philosopher Heraclitus spoke about the **transitory** nature of the world.

A–171

a.—unnecessary

Many philosophers tell us not to worry about **superfluous** things.

Questions

Q–172

GAMUT
[`gæmət] : 範圍

Your Answer _____

_____

Q–173

FLORA
[`florə] : 植物

Your Answer _____

_____

Q–174

DECIDUOUS
[dɪ`sɪdʒʊəs] : 落葉的

Your Answer _____

_____

Correct Answers

A–172

n.—range

Biology is a vast area of study that runs the **gamut** from chemical processes within a single cell to ecosystems that span continents.

A–173

n.—plants

The **flora** of an area has an impact on which animals can live there.

A–174

a.—plants that have leaves that fall at the end of the growing season

In the autumn, the leaves of **deciduous** trees turn yellow, gold, and red before they fall.

Questions

Q–175

RUSTIC
[`rʌstɪk] : 鄉村的

Your Answer _____

_____

Q–176

FOLIAGE
[`folɪɪdʒ] : 葉子（總稱）

Your Answer _____

_____

Q–177

FRIGID
[`frɪdʒɪd] : 寒冷的

Your Answer _____

_____

Correct Answers

A–175

a.—rural

Some people love **rustic** scenes of country life, but other people do not like them.

A–176

n.—leaves

The **foliage** of tall trees can stop light from reaching shorter trees.

A–177

a.—cold

Some crops grow better than others do in **frigid** climates, which is why rye rather than corn is grown in Scandinavia.

Questions

Q–178

GALE
[gel] : 強風

Your Answer _____

Q–179

HOMOGENEOUS
[ˌhoməˈdʒinɪəs] : 同種的

Your Answer _____

Q–180

HYBRID
[ˋhaɪbrɪd] : 經交配種植的

Your Answer _____

Correct Answers

A–178

n.—very high wind
A strong **gale** can do considerable damage to trees and crops.

A–179

a.—matching, similar
It is convenient to manage **homogeneous** crops, but farmers face the loss of an entire field when there is a disease.

A–180

a.—crossbred
A **hybrid** plant can be stronger than either of its "parents."

Questions

Q–181

FALLOW
[`fælo] : 休耕的

Your Answer _____

Q–182

ITINERANT
[aɪ`tɪnərənt] : 漂泊的

Your Answer _____

Q–183

RENOUNCE
[rɪ`naʊns] : 放棄

Your Answer _____

Correct Answers

A–181

a.—unplanted

Many farmers rotate crops from field to field and let some of their land lie **fallow** each year.

A–182

a.—roaming

Some poor farmers in Africa lead an **itinerant** life, farming a piece of land for a few years and then moving on to look for new fields.

A–183

v.—quit

A farmer must **renounce** the use of chemicals for several years before his crops can be called organic.

Questions

Q–184

E. COLI
[ɪˋkoˌlaɪ] : 桿菌

Your Answer _____

Q–185

INVEIGH
[ɪnˋve] : 痛罵

Your Answer _____

Q–186

IRASCIBLE
[ɪˋræsəbl̩] : 暴躁的

Your Answer _____

Correct Answers

A–184

n.—a harmful bacteria
Some people think that organic foods are more likely to carry **E. coli** (Escherichia coli), but others do not support this view.

A–185

v.—denounce
The people who **inveigh** against pesticides and genetically modified crops rarely admit that these things have saved millions of people from starvation.

A–186

a.—irritable
The African honeybee is very **irascible**, and this has earned it the title of "killer bee."

Questions

Q–187

DECLIVITY
[dɪ`klɪvətɪ] : 下坡，傾斜

Your Answer _____

Q–188

MURKY
[`mɝkɪ] : 混濁不清的

Your Answer _____

Q–189

NOVICE
[`nɑvɪs] : 新手，初學者

Your Answer _____

Correct Answers

A–187

n.—slope

On land that has a **declivity**, rain can wash away topsoil.

A–188

a.—unclear

River water can become brown and **murky** when topsoil and fertilizer from large farms get washed into it by rain.

A–189

n.—beginner

Very often, a **novice** at gardening does not realize that different plants need different amounts of water.

Questions

Q–190

BLIGHT
[blaɪt] : 植物病蟲害

Your Answer _____

_____

Q–191

CARDINAL
[`kardṇəl] : 主要的

Your Answer _____

_____

Q–192

DOCILE
[`dɑsḷ] : 溫順的

Your Answer _____

_____

Correct Answers

A–190

n.—plant disease

When orange trees in Florida are hit by **blight**, you know that the price of juice will soon be rising.

A–191

a.—principal

It is of **cardinal** importance for farmers to maintain the quality of their soil.

A–192

a.—gentle

Domestic animals are bred to be **docile**.

Questions

Q–193

IRKSOME
[ˋɝksəm] : 令人厭煩的

Your Answer _____

_____

Q–194

ALIGHT
[əˈlaɪt] : （鳥）停留

Your Answer _____

_____

Q–195

FECUNDITY
[fɪˋkʌndətɪ] : 繁殖力

Your Answer _____

_____

Correct Answers

A–193

a.—annoying

Farmers found that birds were **irksome** pests who ate their corn, so they put scarecrows in their fields to frighten their winged dinner guests away.

A–194

v.—stay

Eventually crows get used to scarecrows and might even **alight** on them.

A–195

n.—productivity

Weather conditions can sometimes affect the **fecundity** of livestock.

Questions

Q–196

HUSBANDRY
[`hʌzbəndrɪ] : 飼養業

Your Answer —————————————————————

Q–197

PREDATORY
['prɛdə,torɪ] : 捕食其他動物的

Your Answer —————————————————————

Q–198

ACCOST
[ə`kɔst][ə`kɑst] : 使面對，對質

Your Answer —————————————————————

Correct Answers

A–196

n.—animal raising
Nowadays, you can study animal **husbandry** in college.

A–197

a.—hunting
In the Midwest, farmers often complain about government regulations that protect **predatory** wild animals that attack their livestock.

A–198

v.—confront
In America, those who fight for animals' rights may **accost** those who seek to injure innocent animals.

Questions

Q–199

COLT
[kolt] : 小馬

Your Answer _____

_____

Q–200

EXTANT
[ˋɛkstənt] [ɪkˋstænt] : 現存的

Your Answer _____

_____

Q–201

SAGACIOUS
[səˋgeʃəs] : 聰敏的

Your Answer _____

_____

Correct Answers

A–199

n.—young horse
Car companies like to name automobiles after fast animals such as the **colt**.

A–200

a.—existing
There are no dinosaurs **extant**, but we can study their relatives, the lizards and the birds.

A–201

a.—intelligent
The elephant always had a reputation for being a **sagacious** animal, and recent scientific research supports this view.

Questions

Q–202

ILLICIT
[ɪˋlɪsɪt] : 不合法的

Your Answer _____

Q–203

BALMY
[ˋbɑmɪ] : 溫和的

Your Answer _____

Q–204

ELUSIVE
[ɪˋlusɪv] : 難以捉摸的

Your Answer _____

Correct Answers

A–202

a.—illegal

African nations are trying to stop the **illicit** trade in ivory from elephants.

A–203

a.—mild

During the winter, many people travel to southern resorts with **balmy** weather to get away from the cold.

A–204

a.—difficult to catch

In recent years, marine biologists have begun to learn more about the **elusive** giant squid.

Questions

Q–205

ESTIMABLE
[ˋɛstəməbḷ] : 可估計的

Your Answer _____

_____

Q–206

FEROCIOUS
[fəˋroʃəs] : 殘暴的

Your Answer _____

_____

Q–207

CLING
[klɪŋ] : 黏住

Your Answer _____

_____

Correct Answers

A–205

a.—calculable

The **estimable** damage that a hurricane causes might be billions of dollars, but some things like human trauma and suffering can never be counted.

A–206

a.—violent

Many species of shark are **ferocious**, but there are a few that are relatively harmless to humans.

A–207

v.—stick to

Scientists have been studying the sticky glue that mussels use to **cling** to rocks and other objects.

Questions

Q–208

TENACIOUSLY
[tɪˋneʃəslɪ] : 不屈不撓地

Your Answer _____

_____

Q–209

ADHESIVENESS
[ədˋhisɪvnɪs] : 黏性

Your Answer _____

_____

Q–210

VERSATILE
[ˋvɝsətḷ] : 多用途的

Your Answer _____

_____

Correct Answers

A–208

adv.—persistently
The glue that a mussel produces through its foot contains a high concentration of an amino acid, which allows it to cling **tenaciously** to wet surfaces.

A–209

n.—stickiness
Unlike the natural glue of mussels, synthetic glue loses its **adhesiveness** when it gets wet.

A–210

a.—all-purpose
Mussel glue would be **versatile** and could be used in many fields.

Questions

Q–211

GRAFT
[græft] : 移植

Your Answer _____

Q–212

COIN
[kɔɪn] : 造（字辭）

Your Answer _____

Q–213

ANOMALOUS
[ə`nɑmələs] : 破例的

Your Answer _____

Correct Answers

A–211

n.—transplant

If successfully developed, mussel glue could be used for tissue **grafts**, medical implants, and dental applications.

A–212

v.—make, invent

Darwin **coined** the term "living fossils" to indicate animals and plants that closely resemble species observed in the fossil record.

A–213

a.—exceptional

Living fossils seem to be a mystery since they are **anomalous** in light of evolutionary theory, and the ginkgo tree is one of them.

Questions

Q–214

THERAPEUTIC
[ˌθɛrəˈpjutɪk] : 治療的

Your Answer _____

Q–215

CONVECTION
[kənˈvɛkʃən] : 對流

Your Answer _____

Q–216

CHAMELEON
[kəˈmiljən] : 變色龍

Your Answer _____

Correct Answers

A–214

a.—healing
Among many **therapeutic** benefits of gingko,
improving memory is probably the best known.

A–215

n.—circulation
Large birds such as eagles can stay aloft for long
periods of time by riding on **convection** currents in
the air.

A–216

n.—lizard that is capable of changing its skin color
Chameleons are best known for their ability to
change color.

Questions

Q–217

DISCERNIBLE
[dɪˋsɚnəbḷ] : 可辨識的

Your Answer _____

Q–218

CAMOUFLAGE
[ˋkæməˌflɑʒ] : 偽裝

Your Answer _____

Q–219

ELONGATE
[ɪˋlɔŋˌget] : 伸長

Your Answer _____

Correct Answers

A–217

a.—observable

The presence of a chameleon is not easily **discernible** because it can change color to match its surroundings.

A–218

v.—disguise

Their ability to change color allows them to **camouflage** themselves.

A–219

v.—stretch out

Chameleons have tongues that they can **elongate** to catch food from a distance.

Questions

Q–220

SYMMETRICAL
[sɪˋmɛtrɪkl̩] : 對稱的

Your Answer _____

Q–221

FICKLE
[ˋfɪkl̩] : 善變的

Your Answer _____

Q–222

AMPHIBIAN
[æmˋfɪbɪən] : 水陸兩棲動物

Your Answer _____

Correct Answers

A–220

a.—balanced

A chameleon's eyes might not appear **symmetrical** because they can look in two directions at the same time.

A–221

a.—changeable

Some studies show that a chameleon changes its color to express its mood; therefore, the word chameleon can also be used to indicate a person who is **fickle**.

A–222

n.—an animal, related to the lizard, that can live in water or on the land

Amphibians such as frogs and toads can live in the water as well as on the land.

Questions

Q–223

TERRESTRIAL
[tə`rɛstrɪəl] : 陸棲的

Your Answer _____

_____

Q–224

VERTEBRATE
[`vɜtə‚bret] : 脊椎動物

Your Answer _____

_____

Q–225

HEREDITY
[hə`rɛdətɪ] : 遺傳

Your Answer _____

_____

Correct Answers

A–223

a.—living on land
Many of them remain **terrestrial** as adults.

A–224

n.—animal that has a skeleton with a spinal column
They are **vertebrates** because they have backbones.

A–225

n.— inheritance
Mendel was the first person who conducted a
scientific study of **heredity**; his work became the
basis of modern genetics.

Questions

Q–226

SIBLING
[`sɪblɪŋ] : 兄弟姐妹

Your Answer _____

Q–227

INTUITIVE
[ɪn`tjʊɪtɪv] : 自然的

Your Answer _____

Q–228

KINDRED
[`kɪndrɪd] : 血緣關係

Your Answer _____

Correct Answers

A–226

n.—brother or sister
Resemblance among **siblings** can be explained by genetic similarities.

A–227

a.—naturally clear to the insight
It seems **intuitive** now to say that there are genetic similarities among family members.

A–228

n.—relatives
In many cultures, **kindred** has always been socially significant, and now it is scientifically important.

Questions

Q–229

PERPETRATOR
[ˋpɝpəˌtretɚ] : 犯罪者

Your Answer _____

_____

Q–230

PROPENSITY
[prəˋpɛnsətɪ] : 傾向

Your Answer _____

_____

Q–231

UNDERPINNING
[ˋʌndɚˌpɪnɪŋ] : 基礎

Your Answer _____

_____

Correct Answers

A–229

n.—criminal
DNA can be used to identify a **perpetrator** and solve a crime that took place a long time ago.

A–230

n.—tendency
Researchers have found a gene that explains why some people have a **propensity** for becoming depressed under stress.

A–231

n.—basis, foundation
Advances in science are providing the **underpinnings** of a new understanding of genetic diseases.

Questions

Q–232

INTRACTABLE
[ɪn`træktəbl̩] : 棘手的

Your Answer _____

Q–233

ONSET
[`ɑnˌsɛt] : 開始

Your Answer _____

Q–234

DISMAL
[`dɪzml̩] : 陰暗的

Your Answer _____

Correct Answers

A-232

a.—stubborn

With more advanced knowledge of genes, doctors will be able to treat **intractable** diseases.

A-233

n.—beginning, start

There are already medicines that can halt the **onset** of some diseases.

A-234

a.—gloomy

Renaissance thinkers thought of the human body as a magnificent structure, but the mystics of the Dark Ages thought of the body as a **dismal** prison.

Questions

Q–235

DILATE
[daɪˋlet][ˋdaɪlet] : **使擴大**

Your Answer _____

Q–236

GASH
[gæʃ] : **割傷**

Your Answer _____

Q–237

INCAPACITATE
[ˌɪnkəˋpæsəˌtet] : **失去能力**

Your Answer _____

Correct Answers

A–235

v.—widen

Certain drugs can make your pupils **dilate**.

A–236

v.—injure, wound

If you fall and **gash** yourself, you should seek medical attention.

A–237

v.—disable

A person can become **incapacitated** by a serious illness.

Questions

Q–238

MAIM
[mem] : 使殘廢

Your Answer

Q–239

TANTALIZE
[ˋtæntḷˌaɪz] : 受引誘，誘惑

Your Answer

Q–240

NAUSEA
[ˋnɔʒə] [ˋnɔziə] [ˋnɔʃə] [ˋnɔsiə] : 反胃想吐

Your Answer

Correct Answers

A–238

v.—disable, cripple

If a farmer is not careful, he can be **maimed** in an accident.

A–239

v.—tempt

Some people are **tantalized** by the idea of improving their looks through plastic surgery.

A–240

n.—upset stomach

Nausea is not uncommon among passengers traveling on ocean-going ships.

Questions

Q–241

UNDULATING
[`ʌndjəˌletɪŋ] : 起伏的

Your Answer _____

Q–242

GAIT
[get] : 步伐

Your Answer _____

Q–243

MALIGNANT
[məˈlɪgnənt] : 惡性的

Your Answer _____

Correct Answers

A–241

a.—rising and falling

The **undulating** waves of the ocean can make people sick until they get used to the movement of the ship.

A–242

n.—walk

A leg injury is likely to affect a person's **gait** for some time.

A–243

a.—dangerous

Malignant tumors should be treated by a doctor as soon as possible.

Questions

Q–244

BLEMISH
[`blɛmɪʃ] : 瑕疵

Your Answer _____

Q–245

MALADY
[`mælədɪ] : 疾病

Your Answer _____

Q–246

DISCRETE
[dɪ`skrit] : 分開的

Your Answer _____

Correct Answers

A–244

n.—imperfection

A **blemish** on the skin is sometimes the sign of a more serious internal illness.

A–245

n.—disease

Acne, a **malady** affecting the skin, is supposed to be made worse by greasy food.

A–246

a.—separate

Scientists say that sleep consists of five **discrete** stages that a person passes through in the course of a night.

Questions

Q–247

ERRATIC
[ɪˋrætɪk] : 不規則的

Your Answer _____

_____

Q–248

PARADOXICAL
[͵pærəˋdɑksɪk!] : 似乎自相矛盾的

Your Answer _____

_____

Q–249

DISRUPT
[dɪsˋrʌpt] : 打斷

Your Answer _____

_____

Correct Answers

A–247

a.—irregular

During the stage of rapid eye movement (REM) sleep, the heart rate speeds up, breathing becomes **erratic** and shallow, and the eyes move rapidly in various directions.

A–248

a.—self-contradictory

REM sleep is also called **paradoxical** sleep because the brain cells behave in a way that resembles the waking state.

A–249

v.—interrupt

After REM sleep is **disrupted**, people do not start over again at Stage 1 sleep but go directly back to REM sleep.

Questions

Q–250

AMNESIA
[æm`niʒɪə] : 健忘

Your Answer _____

_____

Q–251

DEPRIVE
[dɪ`praɪv] : 剝奪

Your Answer _____

_____

Q–252

SLUGGISH
[`slʌgɪʃ] : 遲緩的

Your Answer _____

_____

Correct Answers

A–250

n.—forgetfulness, loss of memory

It is perfectly normal for people to have no memory of the last few minutes before they fall asleep, but people with bouts of **amnesia** should get medical attention.

A–251

v.—take away

When people are **deprived** of sleep, they do not think as clearly as they do when they have enough sleep.

A–252

a.—slow

People who lack sleep usually feel **sluggish**.

Questions

Q–253

SOPORIFIC
[ˌsɑpə`rɪfɪk] : 造成想睡的

Your Answer _____

Q–254

IMPAIR
[ɪm`pɛr] : 傷害，耗損，減弱

Your Answer _____

Q–255

INDULGENT
[ɪn`dʌldʒənt] : 縱容的

Your Answer _____

Correct Answers

A–253

a.—sleep-causing

The herb hops is said to have a mild **soporific** effect, and this is why people who picked it were often considered to be sleepy.

A–254

v.—harm, weaken

A person's mental functioning can be **impaired** because of a lack of sleep.

A–255

a.—liberal, generous

Many people feel they are being overly **indulgent** to themselves by spending eight hours on sleep, but getting a good night's rest is very important.

Questions

Q–256

PREDISPOSITION
[ˌpridɪspə`zɪʃən] : 傾向

Your Answer _____

Q–257

INFLUENZA
[ˌɪnfluˈɛnzə] : 流行性感冒

Your Answer _____

Q–258

PREDOMINANT
[prɪˈdɑmənənt] : 明顯的

Your Answer _____

Correct Answers

A–256

n.—tendency
Some people seem to have a **predisposition** for getting the flu.

A–257

n.—flu
Everybody has had the flu or knows someone who has caught the **influenza** virus, so people sometimes forget that it can be fatal.

A–258

a.—principal, prominent
The most **predominant** symptom of the flu among children is fever.

Questions

Q–259

SCOURGE
[skɝdʒ] : 瘟疫

Your Answer _____

_____

Q–260

RESPIRATORY
[`rɛspərəˌtɔrɪ] : 呼吸的

Your Answer _____

_____

Q–261

CONTAGIOUS
[kən`tedʒəs] : 傳染性的

Your Answer _____

_____

Correct Answers

A–259

n.—plague

More than 20,000 people die from the flu **scourge** every year.

A–260

a.—related to breathing

The flu is a **respiratory** illness that can cause coughs, high fevers, and a runny nose.

A–261

a.—catching, infectious

Flu is caused by viruses, and it is **contagious** since the virus spreads easily from person to person.

Questions

Q–262

PREVALENT
[`prɛvələnt] : 盛行的

Your Answer _____

_____

Q–263

PERVASIVE
[pə`vesɪv] : 普遍的

Your Answer _____

_____

Q–264

VIRULENT
[`vɪrjələnt] : 極毒的，致命的

Your Answer _____

_____

Correct Answers

A–262

a.—prevailing

It can be safer to avoid places where there are crowds when the flu is **prevalent**.

A–263

a.—widespread

There used to be a **pervasive** belief that antibiotics could cure almost anything, even the flu.

A–264

a.—very infectious, deadly

The flu in 1918 first seemed to be a common cold, but the virus turned out to be an especially **virulent** type of influenza.

Questions

Q–265

PANDEMIC
[pæn`dɛmɪk] : 全球流行的疾病

Your Answer _____

_____

Q–266

DEVASTATING
[ˌdɛvəs`tetɪŋ] : 具毀滅性的

Your Answer _____

_____

Q–267

LETHAL
[`liθəl] : 致命的

Your Answer _____

_____

Correct Answers

A–265

n.—huge epidemic
The deadly 1918 flu was a **pandemic** that killed millions around the globe.

A–266

a.—destructive
The 1918 flu was more **devastating** in countries that were weakened by strain and shortages during World War I.

A–267

a.—deadly
Some scientists claim that the **lethal** flu of 1918 was originally a bird flu.

Questions

Q–268

AVIAN
[`evɪən] : 鳥類的

Your Answer _____

Q–269

MUTATE
[`mjutet] : 變化，突變

Your Answer _____

Q–270

STRINGENT
[`strɪndʒənt] : 嚴格的

Your Answer _____

Correct Answers

A–268

a.—of or relating to birds
Avian influenza occurs naturally among birds, but there are reports of human infections.

A–269

v.—change
Researchers believe that avian influenza viruses occasionally **mutate** into a form that will infect humans.

A–270

a.—strict
In 2004, scientists at the Centers for Disease Control and Prevention began research on reconstructing the 1918 influenza virus, and they took **stringent** measures to keep it from escaping the lab.

Questions

Q–271

CONTINGENCY
[kən`tɪndʒənsɪ] : 突發事件

Your Answer _____

Q–272

ANTISEPTIC
[ˌæntə`sɛptɪk] : 殺菌的

Your Answer _____

Q–273

INFLAMMATION
[ˌɪnflə`meʃən] : 發炎

Your Answer _____

Correct Answers

A–271

n.—possible crisis
Nowadays, local health officials need to plan for
contingencies such as bird flu infecting humans.

A–272

a.—antibacterial, antiviral
Washing hands with **antiseptic** soap is one way to
reduce the risk of getting sick during a flu season.

A–273

n.—irritation, swelling
Pinkeye is a common term for an **inflammation** of
the eye.

Questions

Q–274

MEMBRANE
[`mɛmbren] : 膜

Your Answer _____

Q–275

CONTAMINATED
[kən`tæmə͵netɪd] : 弄髒的

Your Answer _____

Q–276

AILMENT
[`elmənt] : 疾病

Your Answer _____

Correct Answers

A–274

n.—tissue layer

Various bacteria and viruses can cause pinkeye and make the **membrane** that covers the white part of the eye turn red for several days.

A–275

a.—dirty

Pinkeye usually occurs in only one eye, but can be easily spread to the other eye by touching it with a **contaminated** hand.

A–276

n.—sickness, illness

Pinkeye is a common **ailment**, but it should not be mistaken for other eye problems.

Questions

Q–277

SPECK
[spɛk] : 斑點

Your Answer _____

Q–278

TEEM
[`tim] : 滿佈，充滿

Your Answer _____

Q–279

DETRIMENTAL
[dɛtrə`mentļ] : 有害的

Your Answer _____

Correct Answers

A–277

n.—spot
Some people get red **specks** in their eyes because
some blood vessels burst during a very strong sneeze.

A–278

v.—overflow, be full of
The world **teems** with bacteria.

A–279

a.—harmful
Many people think of all bacteria as **detrimental** to
health, but there are good bacteria.

Questions

Q–280

INHIBIT
[ɪn`hɪbɪt] : 阻止

Your Answer _____

Q–281

INTESTINAL
[ɪn`tɛstɪnl̩] : 腸的

Your Answer _____

Q–282

CULTURE
[`kʌltʃə] : 培菌

Your Answer _____

Correct Answers

A–280

v.—prevent
Harmful bacteria can cause diseases, but good
bacteria **inhibit** the growth of bad bacteria.

A–281

a.—bowel
We cannot live without beneficial **intestinal** bacteria.

A–282

n.—cultivated bacteria
Many believe that the consumption of live **cultures**
through yogurt promotes good digestion.

Questions

Q–283

PURPORT
[pɚˋpɔrt] : 宣稱

Your Answer _____

Q–284

PASTEURIZE
[ˋpæstʃəˌraɪz] : 高溫殺菌

Your Answer _____

Q–285

SPOILAGE
[ˋspɔɪlɪdʒ] : 腐壞

Your Answer _____

Correct Answers

A–283

v.—claim
Yogurt has been **purported** to strengthen and improve the immune system.

A–284

v.—heat food to kill bacteria
Most milk sold today has been **pasteurized**.

A–285

n.—deterioration
Pasteurization was named after Louis Pasteur, a French chemist, who developed the process while trying to find the cause of wine **spoilage**.

Questions

Q–286

PATHOGENIC
[ˌpæθəˈdʒɛnɪk] : 致病的

Your Answer _____

_____

Q–287

STERILIZE
[ˈstɛrəˌlaɪz] : 殺菌

Your Answer _____

_____

Q–288

ASEPTIC
[əˈsɛptɪk] : 無菌的

Your Answer _____

_____

Correct Answers

A–286

a.—causing disease
The heating process is to kill **pathogenic** bacteria, but it also destroys good bacteria.

A–287

v.—make free from germs and bacteria
When milk is pasteurized, it is not totally **sterilized**.

A–288

a.—free of germs, sterile
Milk processed at an ultrahigh temperature has a shelf life up to six months when it is stored in an **aseptic** package.

Questions

Q–289

DIVERGENT
[də`vɜdʒənt] : 分歧的，不同的

Your Answer _____

Q–290

VIGOROUS
[`vɪgərəs] : 精力充沛的

Your Answer _____

Q–291

PROPONENT
[prə`ponənt] : 支持者，擁護者

Your Answer _____

Correct Answers

A-289

a.—different

There are **divergent** opinions among experts as to whether or not to pasteurize milk at higher temperatures.

A-290

a.—energetic

There are **vigorous** debates about drinking raw milk.

A-291

n.—supporter

Raw milk **proponents** say that the heating process kills good bacteria in milk.

Questions

Q–292

FOREGO
[fɔr`go] : 捨棄

Your Answer _____

Q–293

CONTENTIOUS
[kən`tɛnʃəs]: 具爭議性的

Your Answer _____

Q–294

ONGOING
[`ɑn‚goɪŋ] : 繼續進行的

Your Answer _____

Correct Answers

A-292

v.—do without
Most consumers would not **forego** necessary precautions for food safety just to get a glass of raw milk.

A-293

a.—controversial
The issue of the temperature at which milk should be pasteurized remains **contentious**.

A-294

a.—continuing
The disagreement over raw milk is part of the **ongoing** debate about natural versus processed food.

Questions

Q–295

PREMIER
[`primɪə] : 最初的，最先的

Your Answer _____

Q–296

CONFINE
[kən`faɪn] : 局限

Your Answer _____

Q–297

ADULTERATE
[ə`dʌltəˌret] : 攙雜

Your Answer _____

Correct Answers

A–295

a.—foremost

The U.S. Food and Drug Administration, the nation's **premier** consumer protection and health agency, safeguards public health.

A–296

v.—limit

A century ago federal authority was **confined** to policing imported foods and drugs.

A–297

v.—cheapen, degrade

It was in 1848 that the first national law banned the importation of drugs that were **adulterated**.

Questions

Q–298

DEVIOUS
[`divɪəs] : 不正的，旁門走道的

Your Answer _____

Q–299

CONCOCT
[kən`kɑkt] : 混合調配

Your Answer _____

Q–300

AGITATE
[`ædʒəˌtet] : 激動

Your Answer _____

Correct Answers

A–298

a.—dishonest

In nineteenth-century America, **devious** merchants used to sell nutmeg that was in reality just a piece of wood.

A–299

v.—prepare

Canned foods were **concocted** with chemicals that modified their color.

A–300

v.—disturb

Farmers became **agitated** when they found out that they were facing unfair competition.

Questions

Q–301

CRUSADE
[kru`sed] : 從事活動

Your Answer _____

Q–302

VANGUARD
[`væn͵gɑrd] : 先驅，前鋒

Your Answer _____

Q–303

SPEARHEAD
[`spɪr͵hɛd] : 帶領

Your Answer _____

Correct Answers

A–301

v.—campaign
Dr. Harvey Wiley, a chemist and physician, began to **crusade** for a law for pure food in 1883.

A–302

n.—forefront
Dr. Wiley was in the **vanguard** of the pure food movement.

A–303

v.—lead
Dr. Wiley **spearheaded** the pure food movement, earning him the title of "Father of the Pure Food and Drugs Act."

Questions

Q–304

VEHEMENTLY
[`viəməntlɪ] : 熱切地

Your Answer _____

Q–305

FLAGRANT
[`flegrənt] : 不名譽的

Your Answer _____

Q–306

PRESERVATIVE
[prɪ`zɝvətɪv] : 防腐劑

Your Answer _____

Correct Answers

A–304

adv.—passionately
He **vehemently** promoted keeping the food supply clean.

A–305

a.—shockingly noticeable
Dr. Wiley conducted a five-year study to show that **flagrant** adulteration of food was harmful to public health.

A–306

n.—chemical substance used to keep food from going bad
Dr. Wiley studied which **preservatives** and how much of them would be harmful to humans.

Questions

Q–307

PROHIBIT
[prə`hɪbɪt] : 禁止

Your Answer _____

Q–308

MANDATORY
[`mændə͵torɪ] : 強制性的，義務的

Your Answer _____

Q–309

DISCRETION
[dɪ`skrɛʃən] : 自行斟酌

Your Answer _____

Correct Answers

A–307

v.—forbid
A law in 1906 **prohibited** adulterated and misbranded food and drugs.

A–308

a.—required
Labels listing "Nutrition Facts" are **mandatory** for most processed foods.

A–309

n.—judgment
In the past, serving sizes were left to the **discretion** of the food manufacturers.

Questions

Q–310

NEGLIGIBLE
[`nɛɡlədʒəbl̩] : 極少量的，微不足道的

Your Answer _____

_____

Q–311

CLUTTER
[`klʌtɚ] : 使混亂，造成零亂

Your Answer _____

_____

Q–312

DISCLOSURE
[dɪs`kloʒɚ] : 揭露，宣佈

Your Answer _____

_____

Correct Answers

A–310

a.—tiny, insignificant
Regulations allow manufacturers to use the word "free" when the amount of the nutrient in question is **negligible**.

A–311

v.—mess
Nutrition labels are kept fairly simple because too many facts can **clutter** the label and confuse the consumer.

A–312

n.—uncovering, revelation
In some cases, manufacturers are encouraged to give a complete **disclosure** about their food, even if the label should appear crowded.

Questions

Q–313

EXEMPT
[ɪg`zɛmpt] : 免除的

Your Answer _____

Q–314

AMEND
[ə`mɛnd] : 修改，更正

Your Answer _____

Q–315

OVERSEE
[ovɚ`si] : 監督

Your Answer _____

Correct Answers

A–313

a.—freed, excluded, not required to
Foods served for immediate consumption in restaurants or produced by small businesses are **exempt** from nutrition labeling.

A–314

v.—modify
The Food and Drug Administration (FDA) constantly **amends** its regulations on nutrition labeling.

A–315

v.—supervise
The FDA **oversees** many of the steps a company takes when it develops a new drug.

Questions

Q–316

PETITION

[pə`tɪʃən] : 請求，申請

Your Answer _____

_____

Q–317

IMPLEMENT

[`ɪmpləmənt] : 實行

Your Answer _____

_____

Q–318

CONCUR

[kən`kɝ] : 同意

Your Answer _____

_____

211

Correct Answers

A–316

v.—request
Anyone can **petition** for a change in FDA regulations.

A–317

v.—carry out
Very often, the government gives the industry a fair amount of time to **implement** a new regulation.

A–318

v.—agree
Health officials used to think that trans fats were okay, but now most people **concur** that trans fats are bad for you.

Questions

Q–319

EXPLICITLY
[ɪk`splɪsɪtlɪ] : 清清楚楚地

Your Answer _____

_____

Q–320

RANCID
[`rænsɪd] : 腐壞的，發臭的

Your Answer _____

_____

Q–321

HYDROGENATE
[`haɪdrədʒəˌnet][haɪ`drɑdʒəˌnet] : 使氫化

Your Answer _____

_____

Correct Answers

A–319

adv.—clearly
Since 2006, trans fatty acids have had to be **explicitly** listed on nutrition labels.

A–320

a.—spoiled
Liquid vegetable oils do not stand heat well and become **rancid** quickly.

A–321

v.—add hydrogen to unsaturated fats
Trans fatty acids are formed when liquid vegetable oils are **hydrogenated**.

Questions

Q–322

CLOG
[klɑg] : 阻塞

Your Answer _____

_____

Q–323

UBIQUITOUS
[ju`bɪkwətəs] :無所不在的，到處都是的

Your Answer _____

_____

Q–324

PALATABLE
[`pælətəb!] : 口味合宜的，味道可接受的

Your Answer _____

_____

Correct Answers

A–322

v.—block
Hydrogenated vegetable oil can stay on the shelf longer, but it **clogs** blood vessels.

A–323

a.—everywhere
Food companies are looking for alternatives to the **ubiquitous** yet unhealthy trans fats.

A–324

a.—acceptable (to the taste)
Many people think that without trans fats, foods like french fries are less **palatable**.

Questions

Q–325

CURB
[kɝb] : 限制

Your Answer _____

_____

Q–326

REVERBERATE
[rɪˋvɝbəˌret] : 造成回響

Your Answer _____

_____

Q–327

CONSENSUS
[kənˋsɛnsəs] : 共識，意見一致

Your Answer _____

_____

Correct Answers

v.—restrict
The mayor of New York City asked restaurants to
curb the use of trans fats for the sake of public health.

v.—echo
A ban on using trans fats for restaurants in New York
would **reverberate** throughout the country.

n.—agreement
There is a disagreement on what kind of oil is best
for health, but there seems to be a **consensus** that
hydrogenated vegetable oil is the worst.

Questions

Q–328

UNDERMINE
[ˌʌndəˈmaɪn] : 逐漸損害

Your Answer

Q–329

PARADIGM
[ˈpærəˌdaɪm] : 理論規範

Your Answer

Q–330

LONGEVITY
[lɑnˈdʒɛvətɪ] : 壽命

Your Answer

Correct Answers

A–328

v.—ruin

Most health experts believe that trans fats can **undermine** a person's health in the long run.

A–329

n.—theory

It seems that we always have a new **paradigm** to explain what food is good or bad.

A–330

n.—length of life

The food you eat can affect your **longevity**.

Questions

Q–331

CONGENITAL
[kən`dʒɛnətl̩] : 先天的

Your Answer _____

_____

Q–332

RELAPSE
[`rilæps] [rɪ`læps] : 復發

Your Answer _____

_____

Q–333

INKLING
[`ɪŋklɪŋ] : 略有所知

Your Answer _____

_____

Correct Answers

A–331

a.—occurring at birth

Good nutrition during pregnancy can help prevent **congenital** birth defects.

A–332

n.—return

Good nutrition can prevent a person from having a **relapse** of various diseases.

A–333

n.—clue

Until the twentieth century, people had no **inkling** that there were such things as vitamins.

Questions

Q–334

PREDILECTION
[ˌprɛdəˈlɛkʃən][ˌpridɪˈlɛkʃən] : **偏好**

Your Answer _____

Q–335

ENTICING
[ɪnˈtaɪsɪŋ] : **吸引人的**

Your Answer _____

Q–336

GLAZE
[glez] : **外層**

Your Answer _____

Correct Answers

A–334

n.—preference
Humans have a natural **predilection** for foods that are sweet, fatty, or salty.

A–335

a.—attractive
For some people, nothing is more **enticing** than a big, moist fresh donut and a hot cup of coffee.

A–336

n.—covering, coating
The **glaze** on a donut is mostly sugar.

Questions

Q–337

ENERGIZE
[ˋɛnɚˏdʒaɪz] : 使有精神

Your Answer _____

_____

Q–338

CIRCUMVENT
[ˏsɝkəmˋvɛnt] : 逃避

Your Answer _____

_____

Q–339

RUDIMENTARY
[ˏrudəˋmɛntərɪ] : 基本的

Your Answer _____

_____

Correct Answers

A–337

v.—stimulate

Some people feel **energized** after drinking coffee.

A–338

v.—avoid, go around

High-fructose corn syrup **circumvents** the need to use more expensive cane sugar, but it is more fattening.

A–339

a.—fundamental

Public health experts often put **rudimentary** nutrition advice into a diagram form such as a "food pyramid."

Questions

Q–340

EFFICACY
[ˋɛfəkəsɪ] : 效用

Your Answer _____

_____

Q–341

RESILIENT
[rɪˋzɪlɪənt] : 有耐力的，能抗壓的

Your Answer _____

_____

Q–342

FAMISHED
[ˋfæmɪʃt] : 饑餓的

Your Answer _____

_____

Correct Answers

A–340

n.—effect
Doctors used to doubt the **efficacy** of taking a daily vitamin pill, but now many of them encourage the practice.

A–341

a.—durable
If you eat a healthy diet, your immune system will be strong and **resilient**.

A–342

a.—starving
Some people feel **famished** when they wake up in the morning, while others routinely skip breakfast.

Questions

Q–343

SAVOR
[`sevɚ] : 味道

Your Answer _____

_____

Q–344

ALLEVIATE
[ə`livɪˌet] : 減輕，緩和

Your Answer _____

_____

Q–345

LUBRICANT
[`lubrɪkənt] : 潤滑油

Your Answer _____

_____

Correct Answers

A–343

n.—flavor

A person who is on a diet that is low in salt and fat might use spices to add **savor** to his food.

A–344

v.—relieve

Some nutritionists say that fish oil can help to **alleviate** the discomfort of stiff joints.

A–345

n.—oil

Some people feel taking fish oil is like applying a **lubricant** to their joints.

Questions

Q–346

LOATHE
[loð] : 厭惡

Your Answer _____

Q–347

DETEST
[dɪˋtɛst] : 厭惡

Your Answer _____

Q–348

MINCE
[mɪns]: 切碎

Your Answer _____

Correct Answers

A–346

v.—hate
Some people **loathe** the taste of fish oil.

A–347

v.—hate
Some manufacturers make fish oil with cherry or mint flavor for those who **detest** the taste of fish oil.

A–348

v.—chop into tiny pieces
Health-conscious cooks often **mince** garlic and put it into their food.

Questions

Q–349

PUNGENT
[`pʌndʒənt] : 刺激的，辛辣的

Your Answer

Q–350

PRACTITIONER
[præk`tɪʃənə] : 執業者

Your Answer

Q–351

SALLOW
[`sælo] : 面黃有病的

Your Answer

Correct Answers

A–349

a.—sharp, spicy

Garlic is known for its **pungent** smell and health benefits.

A–350

n.—person who practices a profession

Even some medical **practitioners** do not know much about nutrition.

A–351

a.—sickly

If people are eating poorly, their hair might look dull or they might have a **sallow** complexion.

Questions

Q–352

MORBID
[`mɔrbɪd] : 病態的

Your Answer _____

_____

Q–353

HAMPER
[`hæmpɚ] : 阻礙

Your Answer _____

_____

Q–354

JOLT
[dʒolt] : 震撼

Your Answer _____

_____

Correct Answers

A–352

a.—diseased, unhealthy mental state
Some thin people try to lose weight out of a **morbid** concern with their appearance.

A–353

v.—block
A bad diet can **hamper** one's recovery from illness.

A–354

n.—shock
Some people need an unpleasant **jolt** to motivate them.

Questions

Q–355

ABORTIVE
[ə`bɔrtɪv] : 不成功的

Your Answer _____

Q–356

FLUSTER
[`flʌstə] : 慌亂

Your Answer _____

Q–357

CORPULENT
[`kɔrpjələnt] : 肥胖的

Your Answer _____

Correct Answers

A–355

a.—unsuccessful

A person who makes an **abortive** attempt to lose weight is often worse off than the person who never tried at all.

A–356

v.—disturb

If you tell someone that he is overweight, he might become **flustered** or even angry.

A–357

a.—fat

As people grow older, they often have to eat less if they wish to avoid becoming **corpulent**.

Questions

Q–358

METABOLISM
[mə`tæbḷ͵ɪzəm] : 新陳代謝

Your Answer _____

_____

Q–359

ABSTEMIOUS
[æb`stimɪəs] : 有節制的

Your Answer _____

_____

Q–360

EMACIATED
[ɪ`meʃɪ͵etɪd] : 瘦弱的

Your Answer _____

_____

Correct Answers

A–358

n.—how fast one's body burns food
Many believe that people have a slower **metabolism** as they age, but some researchers disagree with this view.

A–359

a.—moderate, self-denying
Some people adopt an **abstemious** lifestyle to lose weight or regain their health.

A–360

a.—very thin
A person who does not eat enough may have an **emaciated** appearance.

Questions

Q–361

ASPIRE
[ə`spaɪr] : 渴望

Your Answer _____

Q–362

PURGE
[pɜdʒ] : 清洗

Your Answer _____

Q–363

EFFERVESCE
[ˌɛfɚ`vɛs] : 起泡沫

Your Answer _____

Correct Answers

A–361

v.—yearn, hope (for)
Good health is something that many sick people can only **aspire** to, although many of us take it for granted.

A–362

v.—cleanse
Some people go on special diets or drink a lot of mineral water in an attempt to **purge** their systems.

A–363

v.—foam, bubble
Some kinds of mineral water **effervesce** naturally, but the bubbles in soda are always artificial.

Questions

Q–364

FERMENTING
[ˋfɝmɛntɪŋ] : 發酵

Your Answer _____

Q–365

INSOMNIA
[ɪnˋsɑmnɪə] : 失眠

Your Answer _____

Q–366

EMBRACE
[ɪmˋbres] : 包含

Your Answer _____

Correct Answers

A–364

n.—growing

The **fermenting** of yeast causes bread to rise.

A–365

n.—difficulty in falling asleep

Sometimes a person suffering from **insomnia** takes extra calcium before bedtime to help him or her sleep.

A–366

v.—cover, include

Physical science **embraces** a wide range of fields such as astronomy, chemistry, geology, oceanography, and physics.

Questions

Q–367

FLUX
[flʌks] : 變遷

Your Answer _____

Q–368

SUBSIDE
[səb`saɪd] : 平息

Your Answer _____

Q–369

IMPEDIMENT
[ɪm`pɛdəmənt] : 障礙

Your Answer _____

Correct Answers

A–367

n.—change

The stars and planets are in a constant state of **flux**, but since they are so far away, we usually do not notice it.

A–368

v.—calm down

On the surface of our own sun, solar flares periodically erupt and then **subside**.

A–369

n.—obstacle

Space-based telescopes do not suffer from the **impediments** caused by the Earth's atmosphere.

Questions

Q–370

RETROGRADE
[ˋrɛtrəˌgred] : 逆行的

Your Answer

Q–371

GHASTLY
[ˋgæstlɪ] : 驚人的

Your Answer

Q–372

ECCLESIASTICAL
[ɪˌklizɪˋæstɪkḷ] : 教會的

Your Answer

Correct Answers

A–370

a.—backward

At some times of the year, certain planets appear to have a **retrograde** motion.

A–371

a.—terrible

In recent years, we have heard the **ghastly** idea that the dinosaurs were wiped out by a meteor and that we could suffer a similar fate.

A–372

a.—pertaining to the church or clergy

In the Middle Ages, the **ecclesiastical** point of view was that the stars and planets were divine bodies that could never change.

Questions

Q–373

HERETIC
[`hɛrətɪk] : 異教徒，持異端邪論者

Your Answer _____

_____

Q–374

INCREDULITY
[ˌɪnkrə`djulətɪ] : 不相信

Your Answer _____

_____

Q–375

BELIE
[bɪ`laɪ] : 隱藏，使遮蔽

Your Answer _____

_____

Correct Answers

A–373

n.—renegade

Galileo was judged to be a **heretic** because of the things he saw through his telescope.

A–374

n.—disbelief

When Galileo talked about what he observed through his new telescope, people greeted him with **incredulity**.

A–375

v.—hide, make seem false

The familiar twinkling of the stars each night **belies** the fact that much of the starlight we are looking at is millions of years old.

Questions

Q–376

COALESCE
[koə`lɛs] : 接合

Your Answer _____

Q–377

EXTRANEOUS
[ɛk`strenɪəs] : 額外的

Your Answer _____

Q–378

ALACRITY
[ə`lækrətɪ] : 渴望

Your Answer _____

Correct Answers

A–376

v.—combine, come together
Some scientists say that planets come into existence
when clouds of dust in space **coalesce**.

A–377

a.—additional
In an urban setting, **extraneous** light can make it hard
to see the stars.

A–378

n.—eagerness
Some amateur astronomers try with great **alacrity** to
catch glimpses of events like meteor showers.

Questions

Q–379

GENESIS
[`dʒɛnəsɪs] : 起源

Your Answer _____

Q–380

ASTEROID
[`æstəˌrɔɪd] : 小行星

Your Answer _____

Q–381

ANOMALY
[ə`nɑməlɪ] : 反常

Your Answer _____

Correct Answers

A–379

n.—origin
Scientists who seek to understand the **genesis** of stars look to the vast gas clouds where they might form.

A–380

n.—minor planet
Many people do not know that there is a belt of **asteroids** in our solar system.

A–381

n.—exception
People used to describe black holes as **anomalies** in the continuum of time and space.

Questions

Q–382

BEREAVED
[bə`rivd] : 傷心的

Your Answer _____

Q–383

CONGENIAL
[kən`dʒinjəl] : 友善的

Your Answer _____

Q–384

HYPOTHESIZE
[haɪ`paθəˌsaɪz] : 假設，設立理論

Your Answer _____

Correct Answers

A–382

a.—sad

Many enthusiastic stargazers were **bereaved** when they heard that the Hubble Space Telescope might not be repaired.

A–383

a.—friendly

Astrologers believe that Jupiter is a **congenial** planet that brings good fortune.

A–384

v.—theorize

Some scientists **hypothesize** that the dark spots on the moon are the results of ancient volcanic eruptions.

Questions

Q–385

DEARTH
[dɜθ] : 缺乏

Your Answer

Q–386

EMISSARY
[ˋɛmɪˏsɛrɪ] : 使者

Your Answer

Q–387

CELESTIAL
[səˋlɛstʃəl] : 天空的

Your Answer

Correct Answers

A–385

n.—lack

Although scientists have found some evidence that there once was water on Mars, most assume that there is a **dearth** of this life-giving liquid everywhere but on Earth.

A–386

n.—messenger

The planet closest to the sun is called Mercury after the winged **emissary** of the Roman gods.

A–387

a.—heavenly

Pluto, a **celestial** body, was called a planet for more than seventy-five years.

Questions

Q–388

DIVULGE
[də`vʌldʒ] : 洩漏

Your Answer _____

_____

Q–389

RELEGATE
[`rɛləˌget] : 降級

Your Answer _____

_____

Q–390

UPROAR
[`ʌpˌror] : 喧嘩，怒聲

Your Answer _____

_____

Correct Answers

A–388

v.—disclose

Some people hoped Pluto would still remain a planet until the International Astronomical Union **divulged** its decision to demote it.

A–389

v.—lower, demote

Many people felt sad when the International Astronomical Union finally voted to **relegate** Pluto to the status of dwarf planet.

A–390

n.—anger, outcry

Pluto's losing its status as a planet caused an **uproar** among the general public.

Questions

Q–391

JEOPARDY
[ˋdʒɛpədɪ] : 風險

Your Answer _____

Q–392

BIZARRE
[bɪˋzɑr] : 奇特的

Your Answer _____

Q–393

DORMANT
[ˋdɔrmənt] : 靜止不動的

Your Answer _____

Correct Answers

A–391

n.—danger

As a matter of fact, Pluto's status as a planet was in **jeopardy** in the early 1990s when astronomers found objects even larger than Pluto orbiting beyond it.

A–392

a.—odd

Some astronomers think Pluto's orbit is **bizarre** because it rotates in a direction opposite to the other planets.

A–393

a.—inactive

Some astronomers thought Pluto was a **dormant** comet.

Questions

Q–394

DEMOTE
[dɪ`mot] : 降級

Your Answer _____

Q–395

ALIGN
[ə`laɪn] : 成一直線

Your Answer _____

Q–396

OMEN
[`omən] : 預兆

Your Answer _____

Correct Answers

A–394

v.—lower

After astronomers **demoted** Pluto to the status of dwarf planet in 2006, there were only eight planets in our solar system.

A–395

v.—line up

Eclipses occur when the Earth, moon and sun are **aligned** in a row.

A–396

n.—sign

In ancient times, people often thought an eclipse to be a bad **omen**.

Questions

Q–397

DEVOUR
[dɪˋvaʊr] : 吞食

Your Answer

Q–398

FATUOUS
[ˋfætʃʊəs] : 愚蠢可笑的

Your Answer

Q–399

PRESAGE
[ˋprɛsɪdʒ] : 預示

Your Answer

Correct Answers

A–397

v.—eat

There were myths that described an eclipse as a heavenly dog or dragon that **devoured** the sun or moon.

A–398

a.—absurd, silly

With more understanding of modern science, many folktales associated with eclipses are considered **fatuous**.

A–399

v.—predict

There still are people who believe that an eclipse **presages** war.

Questions

Q–400

BEHOLD
[bɪˋhold] : 觀注

Your Answer _____

_____

Q–401

VENERABLE
[ˋvɛnərəb!] : 神聖的

Your Answer _____

_____

Q–402

LUNATIC
[ˋlunəˏtɪk] : 瘋子

Your Answer _____

_____

Correct Answers

A–400

v.—look at

A total solar eclipse is amazing to **behold**, but looking at it directly is harmful to the eyes.

A–401

a.—respected

Today, some cultures continue the **venerable** tradition of holding moon festivals.

A–402

n.—mentally ill person

A full moon was believed to drive a person crazy, as shown in the word **lunatic**, which is derived from lunar.

Questions

Q-403

UNRAVEL
[ʌn`ævl̩] : 解開

Your Answer _____

Q-404

PROBE
[prob] : 探測

Your Answer _____

Q-405

RAPTURE
[`ræptʃɚ] : 欣喜

Your Answer _____

Correct Answers

A–403

v.—solve

Scientific progress has **unraveled** many mysteries of the moon.

A–404

n.—explorer

A lunar **probe** seemed unbelievable in the 1950s although people had dreamed about flying to the moon since ancient times.

A–405

n.—joy

Many people felt **rapture** when the first man landed on the moon in 1969.

Questions

Q–406

CUMBERSOME

[`kʌmbɚˌsəm] : 笨重的

Your Answer _____

_____

Q–407

SIMULATE

[`sɪmjəˌlet] : 模擬

Your Answer _____

_____

Q–408

NULL

[nʌl] : 零的

Your Answer _____

_____

Correct Answers

A–406

a.—bulky

The **cumbersome** space suit that Neil Armstrong wore weighed about 180 pounds.

A–407

v.—imitate

Before their missions, astronauts receive training in settings that **simulate** an actual space flight.

A–408

a.—zero

Astronauts are also trained to work in **null**-gravity conditions.

Questions

Q–409

LOCOMOTION
[ˌlokəˈmoʃən] : 移動

Your Answer

Q–410

TANGIBLE
[ˈtændʒəbḷ] : 實際的

Your Answer

Q–411

ENVISION
[ɪnˈvɪʒən] : 想像，展望

Your Answer

Correct Answers

A–409

n.—movement
Astronauts are trained in an environment designed to teach them how to handle **locomotion** in space.

A–410

a.—actual, real
Opponents of space travel argue that the benefits are not **tangible**, but many beneficial technologies have come from space exploration.

A–411

v.—imagine
The American space agency **envisions** a permanent base on the moon by 2024.

Questions

Q–412

OUTPOST
[`aʊtˌpost] : 基地

Your Answer _____

_____

Q–413

AXIS
[`æksɪs] : 軸線

Your Answer _____

_____

Q–414

EQUINOX
[`ikwəˌnɑks] : 晝夜平分，春分或秋分

Your Answer _____

_____

Correct Answers

A–412

n.—base
It will take some time for astronauts to get used to life on a lunar **outpost**.

A–413

n.—a straight line around which a body rotates or turns
The tilt of the Earth's **axis** makes one hemisphere closer to the sun.

A–414

n.—literally means equal periods of day and night
Equinoxes occur twice a year, in the spring and fall.

Questions

Q–415

VERNAL
[`vɝn!] : 春天的

Your Answer _____

Q–416

GASEOUS
[`gæsɪəs] : 氣體的

Your Answer _____

Q–417

INSULATE
[`ɪnsəˌlet] : 使隔絕

Your Answer _____

Correct Answers

A–415

a.—occurring in spring

The **vernal** equinox is in late March in the Northern Hemisphere.

A–416

a.—existing in a state of gas

The Earth is surrounded by a thin **gaseous** layer, which is called the atmosphere.

A–417

v.—protect

A thin layer of gases **insulates** the Earth against harsh temperature changes.

Questions

Q–418

BANEFUL
[`benfəl] : 有害的

Your Answer _____

Q–419

SUSCEPTIBLE
[sə`sɛptəb!] : 易被影響的

Your Answer _____

Q–420

CONFOUND
[kən`faʊnd] : 使困惑

Your Answer _____

Correct Answers

A–418

a.—harmful

The ozone layer of the atmosphere protects us from **baneful** ultraviolet sunlight.

A–419

a.—vulnerable

Without the protection of the ozone layer, people are more **susceptible** to skin cancer.

A–420

v.—confuse

Many people were **confounded** when they first heard of the thinning of the ozone layer.

Questions

Q–421

SCRUTINIZE
[ˋskrutn͵aɪz] : 詳細察看

Your Answer _____

_____

Q–422

AEROSOL
[ˋɛrə͵sɑl] : 噴霧的

Your Answer _____

_____

Q–423

INSIDIOUSLY
[ɪnˋsɪdɪəslɪ] : 潛伏地 · 暗中地

Your Answer _____

_____

Correct Answers

A–421

v.—examine

Scientists started to **scrutinize** the ozone layer in the 1970s.

A–422

a.—spray

In the 1970s, scientists suggested that the ozone thinning had much to do with chemicals that were used in **aerosol** cans and refrigerators.

A–423

adv.—sneakily

Certain human activities that seem good might **insidiously** destroy the ozone.

Questions

Q–424

DEDUCE
[dɪ`djus] : 推論

Your Answer _____

Q–425

VERIFY
[`vɛrəˌfaɪ] : 證實

Your Answer _____

Q–426

EMISSION
[ɪ`mɪʃən] : 散發物

Your Answer _____

Correct Answers

A–424

v.—infer, conclude

From scientific experiments, researchers are able to **deduce** that increased levels of chlorofluorocarbon (CFC) are thinning the ozone layer.

A–425

v.—confirm

The discovery of the ozone hole **verified** scientists' concerns that certain chemicals might be harmful to the ozone layer.

A–426

n.—release, a substance that is given out

Scientists concluded that the **emission** of harmful chemicals such as CFCs causes the ozone layer to become thinner.

Questions

Q–427

DIMINISH
[də`mɪnɪʃ] : 減少

Your Answer _____

Q–428

DEPLETE
[dɪ`plit] : 使耗減

Your Answer _____

Q–429

POSTULATE
[`pɑstʃəˌlet] : 假設

Your Answer _____

Correct Answers

A–427

v.—decrease
If the ozone layer **diminishes**, more ultraviolet light can reach the Earth's surface.

A–428

v.—reduce
If the ozone layer is completely **depleted**, life on Earth will not be protected from harmful ultraviolet radiation.

A–429

v.— assume
Scientists **postulate** that increased ultraviolet radiation may eventually damage the human immune system.

Questions

Q–430

ERADICATE
[ɪˋrædɪˌket] : 消滅

Your Answer _____

Q–431

PROTOCOL
[ˋprotəˌkəl] : 協議

Your Answer _____

Q–432

AVERT
[əˋvɝt] : 避免

Your Answer _____

Correct Answers

A–430

v.—erase
Without the protection of the ozone layer, life on
Earth would be **eradicated**.

A–431

n.—agreement
In 1987, more than 170 countries signed the Montreal
Protocol to stop making certain substances that might
cause the ozone layer to become thinner.

A–432

v.—avoid
The agreement is an international effort to **avert**
further ozone depletion.

Questions

Q–433

INFLICT
[ɪn`flɪkt] : 致使

Your Answer _____

Q–434

INCONTROVERTIBLE
[ɪnˌkɑntrə`vɜtəb!] : 不容置疑的

Your Answer _____

Q–435

EMINENT
[`ɛmənənt] : 卓越的

Your Answer _____

Correct Answers

A–433

v.—cause
We can minimize the damage **inflicted** by humans.

A–434

a.—undeniable
Chemistry started out almost as a form of magic,
but it slowly changed into a science that demands
incontrovertible proof.

A–435

a.—prominent
Madame Curie was an **eminent** scientist who is
remembered for her work with radium.

Questions

Q–436

DIVISIBILITY
[dəˌvɪzəˋbɪlətɪ] : 可分性

Your Answer _____

_____

Q–437

HARROWING
[ˋhæroɪŋ] : 痛苦的

Your Answer _____

_____

Q–438

CONSPICUOUS
[kənˋspɪkjʊəs] : 顯眼的

Your Answer _____

_____

Correct Answers

A–436

n.—the ability to be split up into smaller parts
When scientists discovered the **divisibility** of the atom into protons, neutrons, and electrons, the way we see the world changed forever.

A–437

a.—difficult
Studying chemistry is a **harrowing** experience for some students.

A–438

a.—obvious
Neon signs are a **conspicuous** sight in most cities after dark.

Questions

Q–439

IMPURITY
[ɪmˋpjʊrətɪ] : 雜質

Your Answer _____

Q–440

FLUFFY
[ˋflʌfɪ] : 鬆軟的

Your Answer _____

Q–441

IMMOBILITY
[ˌɪməˋbɪlətɪ] : 固定不動

Your Answer _____

Correct Answers

A–439

n.—foreign matter

If the sample you are working on in your organic chemistry lab has **impurities** in it, your experiment might fail.

A–440

a.—soft

When the air is cold and dry, snow is **fluffy**.

A–441

n.—lack of motion

We feel that the continents are in an eternal state of **immobility**, but in reality, these huge masses of land are always moving, but very slowly.

Questions

Q–442

PINNACLE
[`pɪnək!] : 頂點

Your Answer _____

_____

Q–443

SUBTERRANEAN
[͵sʌbtə`renɪən] : 地下的，地裡的

Your Answer _____

_____

Q–444

PERTINENT
[`pɝtṇənt] : 相關的

Your Answer _____

_____

Correct Answers

A–442

n.—peak, top

The **pinnacle** of Mount Everest is the highest spot on Earth.

A–443

a.—underground

Underground streams and rivers can make huge **subterranean** caverns.

A–444

a.—relevant

Both the water and the ocean bed are **pertinent** to the field of oceanography.

Questions

Q–445

ABYSS
[ə`bɪs] : 深淵

Your Answer _____

Q–446

AQUEOUS
[`ekwɪəs] : 水的

Your Answer _____

Q–447

ENORMOUSLY
[ɪ`nɔrməslɪ] : 極大的

Your Answer _____

Correct Answers

A–445

n.—hole

Abyss in Greek means a bottomless hole; although the ocean is very deep and some people call it an **abyss**, it certainly has a bottom.

A–446

a.—watery

Just like the land humans live on, the bottom of the ocean has plains, valleys, and mountains, but the **aqueous** environment of the ocean is home to many strange-looking life forms.

A–447

adv.—hugely

The color of the ocean varies **enormously** in different parts of the world, although we usually think of blue as its typical color.

Questions

Q–448

AZURE
[ˋæʒə] : 蔚藍的

Your Answer _____

Q–449

ABSORB
[əbˋsɔrb] : 吸收

Your Answer _____

Q–450

ABUNDANTLY
[əˋbʌndəntlɪ] : 豐富地

Your Answer _____

Correct Answers

A–448

a.—bright blue

The waters of the Atlantic Ocean are gray, but in some parts of the Caribbean, the water is **azure**.

A–449

v.—take in

Water **absorbs** light differently than the air does, which is one reason why colors can look different under water. For example, red could appear black in water.

A–450

adv.—plentifully

Algae grow **abundantly** where there is plenty of water, light and nutrients.

Questions

Q–451

PROFUSE
[prə`fjus] : 豐富的

Your Answer _____

_____

Q–452

PRODIGIOUS
[prə`dɪdʒəs] : 龐大的

Your Answer _____

_____

Q–453

AQUATIC
[ə`kwætɪk] : 水的

Your Answer _____

_____

Correct Answers

A–451

a.—plentiful
Profuse growth of algae in a shallow ocean gives the
water a green color.

A–452

a.—huge
There is a **prodigious** variety of algae although most
people are not interested in it.

A–453

a.—watery
Algae serve as the base of the food chain in **aquatic**
ecosystems.

Questions

Q–454

HABITAT
[`hæbəˌtæt] : 棲息處

Your Answer _____

Q–455

INDISPENSABLE
[ˌɪndɪs`pɛnsəbḷ] : 不可或缺的，必需的

Your Answer _____

Q–456

SYMBIOTIC
[ˌsɪmbi`atɪk][ˌsɪmbaɪ`atɪk] : 共生的

Your Answer _____

303

Correct Answers

A–454

n.—home
The **habitat** for red algae is the deep, cold ocean.

A–455

a.—essential
Algae are **indispensable** to air-breathing life forms since about 75% of the oxygen on Earth is produced by algae.

A–456

a.—mutually beneficial
Coral reefs have a **symbiotic** relationship with algae.

Questions

Q–457

SUSTENANCE
[`sʌstənəns] : 食物

Your Answer _____

_____

Q–458

ENCHANT
[ɪn`tʃænt] : 著迷

Your Answer _____

_____

Q–459

EXPEL
[ɪk`spɛl] : 逐出，趕走

Your Answer _____

_____

Correct Answers

A–457

n.—food

Coral reefs provide shelter to algae; algae provide **sustenance** to coral.

A–458

v.—charm

Many people are **enchanted** by the beautiful color of coral, but the color actually comes from algae.

A–459

v.—force away, force out

Some scientists think that unusually warm temperatures caused coral to **expel** algae and look bleached.

Questions

Q–460

STRAIN
[stren] : 品種，種類

Your Answer _____

_____

Q–461

SMOTHER
[`smʌðə] : 使窒息

Your Answer _____

_____

Q–462

STIFLE
[`staɪfl̩] : 使窒息

Your Answer _____

_____

Correct Answers

A–460

n.—variety, kind
Scientists recently have found that some new **strains**
of algae seem to adapt to warmer temperatures and
save coral reefs.

A–461

v.—suffocate
Coral needs clean water; pollutants can **smother**
coral reefs.

A–462

v.—suffocate
Too much growth of algae can **stifle** coral reefs
because coral also needs sunlight.

Questions

Q–463

HAZARDOUS
[`hæzədəs] : 危險的

Your Answer _____

_____

Q–464

INCESSANT
[ɪn`sɛsn̩t] : 不停的

Your Answer _____

_____

Q–465

DAZZLING
[`dæzl̩ɪŋ] : 亮麗的

Your Answer _____

_____

Correct Answers

A–463

a.—dangerous

Some chemicals that enter seawater are **hazardous** to coral reefs.

A–464

a.—unending

Over thousands of years, the slow yet **incessant** action of glaciers can change the face of a continent.

A–465

a.—beautiful

We associate glaciers with the frozen north, but we should not forget the aurora borealis, the **dazzling** northern lights.

Questions

Q–466

DESOLATE
[`dɛsḷɪt] : 荒蕪的

Your Answer _____

_____

Q–467

DEVOID
[dɪˋvɔɪd] : 缺少的

Your Answer _____

_____

Q–468

ARID
[ˋærɪd] : 乾燥的

Your Answer _____

_____

Correct Answers

A–466

a.—bare, lifeless

Deserts usually appear **desolate**, but actually different species of plants, animals, and insects live there.

A–467

a.—lacking

The Sahara Desert might seem to be **devoid** of all life, but there are some plants and animals that can survive there.

A–468

a.—dry

The **arid** climate of a desert can take centuries to form.

Questions

Q–469

SCANT

[skænt] : 稀少的，不足的

Your Answer _____

Q–470

BARREN

[ˋbærən] : 無生命的

Your Answer _____

Q–471

PRECIPITATION

[prɪˌsɪpəˋteʃən] : 降雨量

Your Answer _____

Correct Answers

A–469

a.—scarce, insufficient
Scant rainfall makes an area dry.

A–470

a.—lifeless
Very often, the formation of a **barren** desert is considered to be caused by a lack of rainfall.

A–471

n.—rainfall
Nevertheless, low **precipitation** alone does not necessarily make an area a desert.

Questions

Q–472

DEGRADATION
[ˌdɛgrəˈdeʃən] : 退化

Your Answer

Q–473

EROSION
[ɪˈroʒən] : 侵蝕

Your Answer

Q–474

DETERIORATE
[dɪˈtɪrɪəˌret] : 惡化

Your Answer

Correct Answers

A–472

n.—decline
It was not until the mid-twentieth century that desertification, the process of the **degradation** of drylands, received serious attention.

A–473

n.—washing away
Much of Iceland suffers from soil **erosion**.

A–474

v.—worsen
Some believe that since humans can make the environment **deteriorate**, they should be able to make it better, too.

Questions

Q–475

ACCELERATE
[æk`sɛləˌret] : 加速

Your Answer _____

_____

Q–476

IRRIGATION
[ˌɪrə`geʃən] : 灌溉

Your Answer _____

_____

Q–477

CONCURRENT
[kən`kɝrənt] : 同時發生的

Your Answer _____

_____

Correct Answers

A–475

v.—speed up

Human activity has **accelerated** the formation of deserts.

A–476

n.—watering

Harmful human activities include overpopulation, overgrazing, and mismanagement of **irrigation**.

A–477

a.—occurring at the same time

It is estimated that there are 1,800 **concurrent** thunderstorms at any given second on Earth.

Questions

Q–478

EMERGENCE
[ɪˋmɝdʒəns] : 出現

Your Answer _____

_____

Q–479

DISCHARGE
[dɪsˋtʃɑrdʒ] : 釋放

Your Answer _____

_____

Q–480

ADVENT
[ˋædvɛnt] : 來臨

Your Answer _____

_____

Correct Answers

A–478

n.—coming forth
Probably because thunderstorms occur so often,
people do not pay much attention to their **emergence**.

A–479

n.—release
Lightning, a natural electrostatic **discharge** produced
by thunderstorms, kills more people each year than
hurricanes or tornadoes.

A–480

n.—coming
Distant thunder can announce the **advent** of an
electrical storm.

Questions

Q–481

ELAPSE
[ɪˋlæps]：**（時間）經過**

Your Answer _____

_____

Q–482

ATMOSPHERIC
[ˌætməsˋfɛrɪk][ˌætməsˋfɪrɪk]：**大氣的**

Your Answer _____

_____

Q–483

ASCERTAIN
[ˌæsɚˋten]：**確實知道**

Your Answer _____

_____

Correct Answers

A–481

v.—pass

Count the seconds that **elapse** between a lightning strike and thunderclap, divide the number by 5, and you will know how many miles you are from the lightning.

A–482

a.—climatic

Thunder can be heard at a maximum distance of ten miles under most **atmospheric** conditions.

A–483

v.—make certain

Of course, you want to **ascertain** that you are in a safe place and stay away from electrical outlets before you do the counting.

Questions

Q–484

SIMULTANEOUSLY
[ˌsaɪmlˈtenɪəslɪ] : 同個時候地

Your Answer _____

Q–485

FACET
[ˈfæsɪt] : 平面

Your Answer _____

Q–486

GEM
[dʒɛm] : 珠寶

Your Answer _____

Correct Answers

A–484

adv.—at the same time
If the lightning and thunder seem to happen
simultaneously, you are pretty close to where the
lightning is.

A–485

n.—side
Diamonds have **facets** like a soccer ball.

A–486

n.—precious stone
A diamond is an expensive **gem**, but it has many
industrial applications, too.

Questions

Q–487

TINT
[tɪnt] : 色彩

Your Answer _____

Q–488

SYNTHETIC
[sɪn`θɛtɪk] : 人造的

Your Answer _____

Q–489

CHARACTERISTIC
[ˌkærəktə`rɪstɪk] : 特質

Your Answer _____

Correct Answers

A–487

n.—color
The most expensive diamonds are clear and without noticeable **tint**.

A–488

a.—artificial
Many diamonds that are used for industrial applications are **synthetic**.

A–489

n.—feature
Artificially made diamonds have **characteristics** similar to natural diamonds.

Questions

Q–490

DISPERSION
[dɪ`spɝ ʃən] : 散開

Your Answer _____

Q–491

LUSTER
[`lʌstɚ] : 光澤

Your Answer _____

Q–492

ABRASIVE
[ə`bresɪv] : 磨擦器

Your Answer _____

Correct Answers

A–490

n.—scattering
Diamonds display a high **dispersion** of light.

A–491

n.—shine
Diamonds keep their **luster** even if you try to scratch them.

A–492

n.—a material that is used to scratch or scrub
Diamonds can be used as **abrasives** because nothing can scratch them but other diamonds.

Questions

Q–493

ENGRAVE
[ɪn`grev] : 雕刻

Your Answer _____

Q–494

THERMAL
[`θɝml̩] : 熱的

Your Answer _____

Q–495

REFRACT
[rɪ`frækt] : 折射

Your Answer _____

Correct Answers

A–493

v.—carve
Diamonds can be used to drill holes in hard beads or to **engrave** other precious stones.

A–494

a.—relating to heat
A diamond is an excellent **thermal** conductor and is used in semiconductor manufacturing to prevent overheating problems.

A–495

v.—bend
Light **refracts** as it passes from one medium to another since light travels at different speeds through different substances.

Questions

Q–496

INTERFACE
[ˋɪntəˌfes] : 接觸面

Your Answer

Q–497

OBLIQUE
[oˋblik][oˋblaɪk] : 斜的

Your Answer

Q–498

COMPRESS
[kəmˋprɛs] : 壓縮

Your Answer

Correct Answers

A–496

n.—the place or boundary between two things
Refraction of light happens at the **interface** where
two different media meet.

A–497

a.—obtuse
A pencil in a glass of water seems to form an **oblique**
angle.

A–498

v.—press together, compact
Sound is produced when air gets **compressed**,
causing a sound wave.

Questions

Q–499

VELOCITY
[vəˈlɑsətɪ] : 速度

Your Answer _____

Q–500

PROPAGATE
[ˈprɑpəˌget] : 傳導

Your Answer _____

Q–501

DISTILLED
[dɪsˈtɪld] : 蒸餾的

Your Answer _____

Correct Answers

A–499

n.—speed

Sound **velocity** is a scientific term to refer to the speed of sound.

A–500

v.—travel

The speed of sound depends on the medium through which sound waves **propagate**. Sound waves travel faster in water than in air.

A–501

a.—purified

Experiments have shown that sound travels much faster in **distilled** water than in ocean water.

Questions

Q–502

OSCILLATE
[`ɑslˌet] : 使振動，來回搖擺

Your Answer _____

Q–503

VIBRATION
[vaɪˋbreʃən] : 振動，來回搖擺

Your Answer _____

Q–504

PENDULUM
[ˋpɛndʒələm] : 鐘擺，搖錘

Your Answer _____

Correct Answers

A–502

v.—move back and forth
Longer and thicker strings **oscillate** more slowly than
shorter and thinner ones do.

A–503

n.—the act of moving back and forth
Faster **vibrations** produce a higher pitch than slower
vibrations.

A–504

n.—swinging weight
A **pendulum** with a longer string takes longer to
swing than a **pendulum** with a shorter string does.

Questions

Q–505

INVERSE
[ɪn`vɝs] [`ɪnvɝs] : 顛倒的

Your Answer _____

Q–506

RESONANT
[`rɛzənənt] : 引起回響的，共鳴的

Your Answer _____

Q–507

ACOUSTIC
[ə`kustɪk] : 音質的

Your Answer _____

Correct Answers

A–505

a.—reverse

There is an **inverse** relationship between the length of a string and the frequency at which it swings. A longer string produces a lower frequency than a shorter string.

A–506

a.—resounding

A viola and a violin look similar although a viola is longer and wider. The sound a viola produces is more **resonant**.

A–507

a.—relating to the quality of sound

There are two f-shaped holes on the front of a violin, and they have very important **acoustic** roles.

Questions

Q–508

INTRIGUE
[ɪn`trig] : 深深吸引

Your Answer _____

Q–509

RENOWNED
[rɪ`naʊnd] : 有名的，有聲譽的

Your Answer _____

Q–510

NOTED
[`notɪd] : 有名的，知名的

Your Answer _____

Correct Answers

A–508

v.—interest greatly

The workings of the violin have **intrigued** some famous physicists.

A–509

a.—famous, acclaimed

Violins from **renowned** makers are very expensive.

A–510

a.—famous

Violins are now mass-produced, but their quality simply can't compare with the old ones from **noted** makers.

Questions

Q–511

HARMONIOUS
[hɑr`monɪəs] : 和諧的，悦耳的

Your Answer _____

_____

Q–512

PERCUSSION
[pɚ`kʌʃən] : 打擊樂器

Your Answer _____

_____

Q–513

STOUT
[staʊt] : 堅固的

Your Answer _____

_____

Correct Answers

A–511

a.—in tune, pleasant
When two piano keys separated by one octave are played at the same time, the sound will be **harmonious**.

A–512

n.—the striking of one object against another
Most people just think of drums when they hear the word **percussion** and overlook the fact that piano strings are hit by small hammers.

A–513

a.—strong, sturdy
The **stout** wood and thick metal of a piano make it too heavy for one person to lift.

Questions

Q–514

CACOPHONOUS
[kə`kɑfənəs] : 音調不調和的

Your Answer _____

Q–515

EXCRUCIATING
[ɪk`skruʃˌʟetɪŋ] : 痛苦的

Your Answer _____

Q–516

IMPEDE
[ɪm`pid] : 妨礙

Your Answer _____

Correct Answers

A–514

a.—unpleasant sounding

Orchestra members must tune their instruments together; otherwise, the music they produce could be **cacophonous**.

A–515

a.—painful

Listening to music produced by a beginner or a bad player can be **excruciating**.

A–516

v.—interfere

Some people think listening to music helps them study, but others find music **impedes** their concentration.

Questions

Q–517

EMANATE
[`ɛmə‚net] : 散出

Your Answer _____

Q–518

IMPERMEABLE
[ɪm`pɜmɪəbḷ] : 不能滲透的

Your Answer _____

Q–519

PROXIMITY
[prɑk`sɪmətɪ] : 附近

Your Answer _____

Correct Answers

A–517

v.—come out
We do not expect sound to **emanate** from a soundproof room.

A–518

a.—impassable
A soundproof room is **impermeable** to sound.

A–519

n.—nearness
People who live in close **proximity** to an airport have to put up with the noise of planes.

Questions

Q–520

ELIMINATE
[ɪˋlɪməˌnet] : 消除

Your Answer _____

_____

Q–521

ABATE
[əˋbet] : 減少

Your Answer _____

_____

Q–522

ATTENUATE
[əˋtɛnjʊˌet] : 使減弱

Your Answer _____

_____

Correct Answers

A–520

v.—remove, get rid of

There is probably no way for airports to **eliminate** noise from airplanes, but there are things they can do to minimize the environmental damage.

A–521

v.—diminish

Boston's Logan Airport works with local communities to **abate** noise from the planes.

A–522

v.—weaken

Keeping windows closed or making sure that doors are shut tight can also **attenuate** noise from outside.

Questions

Q–523

IMPROVIDENT
[ɪm`prɑvədənt] :無遠見的，不經考慮的

Your Answer _____

Q–524

DILUTE
[daɪ`lut][dɪ`lut] : 沖淡，稀釋

Your Answer _____

Q–525

RESIDUE
[`rɛzəˌdu][`rɛzəˌdju] : 殘留

Your Answer _____

Correct Answers

A–523

a.—thoughtless

Careless dumping of chemicals is **improvident** since cleaning up a toxic mess is much more difficult than preventing one.

A–524

v.—thin

If harmful chemicals are dumped into water, they become **diluted**, but they can still be very dangerous.

A–525

n.—leavings, leftovers

Chemical **residues** in the soil can be washed into rivers by rainfall.

Questions

Q–526

LEACH
[litʃ] : 滲漏

Your Answer _____

_____

Q–527

DIFFUSION
[dɪ`fjuʒən] : 擴散

Your Answer _____

_____

Q–528

INCREMENT
[`ɪnkrəmənt] : 增加

Your Answer _____

_____

Correct Answers

A–526

v.—leak

Chemicals and bacteria can **leach** from garbage dumps into groundwater.

A–527

n.—spread

The **diffusion** of car exhaust into the upper atmosphere contributes to global warming.

A–528

n.—increase

Over the past few decades, our planet has grown warmer in slow **increments**.

Questions

Q–529

ANNIHILATE
[ə`naɪəˌlet] : 消滅

Your Answer _____

_____

Q–530

REBUT
[rɪ`bʌt] : 駁斥

Your Answer _____

_____

Q–531

CLAMOR
[`klæmɚ] : 大吵大鬧

Your Answer _____

_____

Correct Answers

A–529

v.—destroy

Some people fear that global warming and pollution will **annihilate** human life from our planet.

A–530

v.—refute

A few scholars **rebut** the claim that there can be no progress without pollution.

A–531

v.—cry out, shout

People are likely to **clamor** if they hear that a garbage dump is going to be put in their town.

Questions

Q–532

ANIMOSITY
[ˌænəˈmɑsətɪ] : 敵意

Your Answer _____

Q–533

RECEPTIVE
[rɪˈsɛptɪv] : 願接納的

Your Answer _____

Q–534

DEFIANT
[dɪˈfaɪənt] : 不服從的

Your Answer _____

Correct Answers

A–532

n.—hostility
There can be considerable **animosity** between environmentalists and industrialists.

A–533

a.—open, accepting
Not all companies are **receptive** to the possibility of tighter government pollution controls.

A–534

a.—disobedient
Some automobile makers gladly follow new pollution guidelines, but others are **defiant**.

Questions

Q–535

HAZY
[`hezɪ] : 朦朧的

Your Answer _____

Q–536

REFRAIN
[rɪ`fren] : 克制，避免

Your Answer _____

Q–537

SURMISE
[sə`maɪz] : 猜測

Your Answer _____

Correct Answers

A–535

a.— unclear

The sky over Los Angeles often looks **hazy** because of all the pollution coming from cars.

A–536

v.— avoid, do without

Drivers can help reduce pollution if they **refrain** from leaving their car engines running while parked.

A–537

v.—guess

We do not know when it will happen, but we can **surmise** that gasoline-powered cars will be replaced by something better.

Questions

Q–538

PINPOINT
[`pɪnˏpɔɪnt] : 指出

Your Answer

Q–539

ANIMATED
[`ænəˏmetɪd] : 動畫的

Your Answer

Q–540

ACRONYM
[`ækrənɪm] : 字首縮寫語

Your Answer

Correct Answers

A–538

v.— identify, locate

Some drivers have a difficult time finding a new place even if they can **pinpoint** the location on a map.

A–539

a.—active, moving

Some people find driving easier with **animated**, three-dimensional maps.

A–540

n.—a word formed by combining the initial letters of a series of words

Radar is commonly used as a word, but it is an **acronym** for radio detecting and ranging.

Questions

Q–541

APPARATUS
[ˌæpəˈretəs] : 儀器

Your Answer _____

_____

Q–542

METICULOUSLY
[məˈtɪkjələslɪ] : 小心翼翼地

Your Answer _____

_____

Q–543

SQUALL
[skwəl] : 大風暴

Your Answer _____

_____

Correct Answers

A–541

n.—equipment
Radar **apparatus** can detect the distance as well as the direction of an object.

A–542

adv.—very carefully
Even though satellites can **meticulously** photograph the Earth's surface, radar is still very important.

A–543

n.—storm, tempest
Weather radar can detect an approaching **squall** and warn airplane pilots.

Questions

Q–544

INTREPID
[ɪn`trɛpɪd] : 勇猛無畏的

Your Answer _____

Q–545

TAMPER
[`tæmpɚ] : 隨意改變

Your Answer _____

Q–546

ENIGMA
[ɪ`nɪgmə] : 謎

Your Answer _____

Correct Answers

A–544

a.—bold

Nowadays, not even the most **intrepid** airline pilot will fly without help from radar stations.

A–545

v.—alter, fool with

Never **tamper** with radar equipment unless you know what you are doing.

A–546

n.—puzzle

Occasionally ships in the Bermuda Triangle have vanished off the radar screen, leaving an **enigma** for researchers.

Questions

Q–547

PERPETUAL
[pə`pɛtʃʊəl] : 永久的

Your Answer _____

_____

Q–548

EQUILIBRIUM
[ˌikwə`lıbrıəm] : 平衡

Your Answer _____

_____

Q–549

SCINTILLA
[sɪn`tɪlə] : 些微

Your Answer _____

_____

Correct Answers

A–547

a.—everlasting
In past centuries, many people tried to create **perpetual**-motion machines.

A–548

n.—balance
Whether you are thinking about high pressures or high temperatures, it is helpful to remember that all systems tend towards **equilibrium** whenever they can.

A–549

n.—trace
Two hundred years ago, nobody had the slightest **scintilla** of doubt that technology would make life better, but people today are not as sure.

Questions

Q–550

DEGENERATE
[dɪ`dʒɛnəˌret] : 退步

Your Answer _____

_____

Q–551

IRREFUTABLE
[ɪrɪ`fjutəbl̩][ɪ`rɛfjutəbl̩] : 不能反駁的

Your Answer _____

_____

Q–552

SANITY
[`sænətɪ] : 神智清楚

Your Answer _____

_____

Correct Answers

A–550

v.—worsen
Some feel that a culture **degenerates** when most people have no idea how its technology works.

A–551

a.—inarguable
There is an **irrefutable** argument for why wind power is better than nuclear power: it costs less.

A–552

n.—soundness, healthy mind
Sometimes people question the **sanity** of an inventor with big dreams.

Questions

Q–553

ENCUMBER
[ɪn`kʌmbɚ] : 負荷，受牽累

Your Answer _____

Q–554

REPLENISH
[rɪ`plɛnɪʃ] : 重新補充，添加

Your Answer _____

Q–555

CASCADING
[kæs`kedɪŋ] : 使如瀑布般的

Your Answer _____

Correct Answers

A–553

v.—burden

With the coming of wireless communication, our telephone system does not have to be **encumbered** by miles of phone cable.

A–554

v.—refill

Since there is no way to **replenish** our supply of certain metals, we recycle them.

A–555

a.—overflowing

Nowadays, a power outage can have a **cascading** effect, with more and more areas losing electricity.

Questions

Q–556

GRID
[grɪd] : **(高壓輸電)線路網**

Your Answer _____

Q–557

VANDALISM
[ˋvændḷ͵ɪzm̩] : 任意破壞

Your Answer _____

Q–558

SABOTAGE
[ˋsæbə͵tɑʒ] : 蓄意毀壞

Your Answer _____

Correct Answers

A–556

n.—power system
In the wake of the blackout in the Northeastern U.S. in 2003, some experts said that the nation's power **grid** must be modernized.

A–557

n.—destructive behavior
The power grid enables electricity generated in one location to be sent to a distant area, but it also allows local damage from storms or **vandalism** to affect the entire system.

A–558

n.—deliberately destructive attack
The 2003 blackout made many realize that an instance of local **sabotage** might harm the whole nation.

Questions

Q–559

DEPLOY
[dɪˋplɔɪ]：部署，安排配置

Your Answer _____

Q–560

PREDICAMENT
[͵prɪˋdɪkəmənt]：為難的處境

Your Answer _____

Q–561

DEMISE
[dɪˋmaɪz]：結束

Your Answer _____

Correct Answers

A–559

v.—arrange

Many states began to develop and **deploy** security plans for their power grids.

A–560

n.—dilemma

Securing the national power system with limited funding presents a **predicament** for government officials.

A–561

n.—end

The transistor caused the **demise** of the vacuum tube.

Questions

Q–562

FUSION
[`fjuʒən] : 融合

Your Answer _____

_____

Q–563

PROLIFERATION
[prəˌlɪfə`reʃən] : 成長；擴散

Your Answer _____

_____

Q–564

INURE
[ɪn`jʊr] : 使習慣於

Your Answer _____

_____

Correct Answers

A–562

n.—uniting, unification
Some people think that we will be able to use nuclear **fusion** as a source of power in a few decades.

A–563

n.—growth
The past decades have witnessed a **proliferation** of both social problems and social scientific theories that seek to explain them.

A–564

v.—accustom
Many Americans are **inured** to the slow nature of their government since their freedoms are safeguarded.

Questions

Q–565

ALLOT
[ə`lɑt] : 分配

Your Answer _____

Q–566

INNATE
[ɪn`net] : 天賦的

Your Answer _____

Q–567

ACCOMMODATE
[ə`kɑmə͵det] : 有調整空間

Your Answer _____

Correct Answers

A–565

v.—assign

The Constitution **allots** power to three different branches of the American Government in a system of checks and balances.

A–566

a.—inherent

In the Declaration of Independence, Thomas Jefferson states that individuals have some **innate** rights.

A–567

v.—make room for

The Constitution of the United States is flexible enough to **accommodate** changing times.

Questions

Q–568

APPREHENSIVE
[æprɪˋhɛnsɪv] : 擔憂的

Your Answer _____

_____

Q–569

ARISTOCRAT
[əˋrɪstəˏkræt] : 貴族

Your Answer _____

_____

Q–570

DELINEATE
[dɪˋlɪnɪˏet] : 描繪

Your Answer _____

_____

Correct Answers

A–568

a.—fearful

After the American Revolution, many of the thirteen former colonies were **apprehensive** about surrendering their rights to a strong central government.

A–569

n.—noble

Some Americans thought that George Washington should be made a king, but he turned down the idea since he did not want to create a government of **aristocrats**.

A–570

v.—outline

The famous Federalist Papers **delineated** a form of government where powers would be split between individual states and the national government.

Questions

Q–571

CREDENCE
[`kridəns] : 信任

Your Answer _____

Q–572

LABYRINTHINE
[ˌlæbə`rɪnθɪn] : 迷宮般的

Your Answer _____

Q–573

DIGRESS
[daɪ`grɛs] : 轉移

Your Answer _____

Correct Answers

A–571

n.—trust, confidence

Few people nowadays give **credence** to George Washington's advice that we should avoid political parties.

A–572

a.—complicated

The more powerful a nation, the more **labyrinthine** its politics becomes.

A–573

v.—depart, wander

When a public figure **digresses** from a topic under discussion, you know that he does not want to talk about it.

Questions

Q–574

GUISE
[gaɪz] : 偽裝

Your Answer _____

Q–575

IMPROMPTU
[ɪm`prɑmptju] : 即席的

Your Answer _____

Q–576

ACCUMULATE
[ə`kjumjəˌlet] : 累積

Your Answer _____

Correct Answers

A–574

n.—pretense

Some people think that "pork-barrel" projects are bribes in the **guise** of government grants.

A–575

a.—unrehearsed

One of the traits of a good leader is the ability to make an effective **impromptu** speech.

A–576

v.—gather

Over the years, the executive branch of government has **accumulated** more and more power.

Questions

Q–577

INSINUATE
[ɪn`sɪnjʊˌet] : 暗示

Your Answer _____

_____

Q–578

IMPROPRIETY
[ˌɪmprə`praɪətɪˌ] : 不得當

Your Answer _____

_____

Q–579

ALLOCATE
[`æləˌket] : 分配

Your Answer _____

_____

Correct Answers

A–577

v.—imply

In the British Parliament, you cannot directly insult a member, but you can **insinuate** some very bad things if you are careful with your words.

A–578

n.—inappropriateness

A small **impropriety** can end a politician's career.

A–579

v.—distribute

Congress has the power to **allocate** funds for different government projects.

Questions

Q–580

DEMAGOGUE
[`dɛməgɑg][`dɛməgɔg]：煽動群眾的政治家

Your Answer _____

Q–581

GARNER
[`gɑrnɚ]：獲得

Your Answer _____

Q–582

PONDEROUS
[`pɑndərəs]：笨重的

Your Answer _____

Correct Answers

A–580

n.—agitator
Many people think that the Depression-era Louisiana Senator Huey Long was a **demagogue** who would say anything to gain power.

A–581

v.—acquire
Before he became president, Lyndon Johnson **garnered** the reputation of being a highly effective leader of the U.S. Senate.

A–582

a.—bulky
Some laws are **ponderous** documents that can be more than 1,000 pages long.

Questions

Q–583

ENRAGE
[ɪn`redʒ] : 憤怒

Your Answer _____

_____

Q–584

RATIFY
[`rætəˌfaɪ] : 批准，認可

Your Answer _____

_____

Q–585

AUSTERITY
[ə`stɛrətɪ] : 嚴格

Your Answer _____

_____

Correct Answers

A–583

v.—anger
Members of Congress can become **enraged** if they feel that the president is sidestepping their authority.

A–584

v.—confirm
The United States Senate must **ratify** all treaties signed by the president.

A–585

n.—severity
When governments practice **austerity**, many programs can lose funding.

Questions

Q–586

JURISDICTION
[dʒʊrɪsˋdɪkʃən] : 司法權

Your Answer _____

Q–587

BRAWL
[brɔl] : 爭吵

Your Answer _____

Q–588

PRESUMPTION
[prɪˋzʌmpʃən] : 假設

Your Answer _____

Correct Answers

A–586

n.—authority
In the United States, Congress has **jurisdiction** over trade between states.

A–587

v.—fight
In the nineteenth century, farmers in the American West would **brawl** over water rights.

A–588

n.—assumption
The **presumption** that a person is innocent until proven guilty is an important part of the American legal system.

Questions

Q–589

IMPARTIAL
[ɪm`pɑrʃəl] : 不偏不倚的

Your Answer _____

_____

Q–590

ACQUIT
[ə`kwɪt] : 洗刷罪名，宣判無罪

Your Answer _____

_____

Q–591

ABSOLVE
[əb`sɑlv] : 洗刷罪名

Your Answer _____

_____

Correct Answers

A–589

a.—unbiased

A judge is supposed to be **impartial**.

A–590

v.—declare innocence

A person who has been found guilty in a lower court might be **acquitted** in a higher court.

A–591

v.—clear

When people are **absolved** of guilt in a criminal trial, their reputations might still be ruined due to media coverage.

Questions

Q–592

VINDICATE
[`vɪndəˌket] : 證明無辜

Your Answer _____

_____

Q–593

ACCOMPLICE
[ə`kamplɪs] : 共犯

Your Answer _____

_____

Q–594

CONSPIRE
[kən`spaɪr] : 圖謀

Your Answer _____

_____

Correct Answers

A–592

v.—prove innocence
Even when a person is **vindicated** in court, his reputation might still be damaged.

A–593

n.—helper
In many cases, an **accomplice** is considered just as guilty as the person who actually commits the crime.

A–594

v.—plot
It is a serious crime to **conspire** against the government.

Questions

Q–595

EMBEZZLE
[ɪmˋbɛzl̩] : 盜用

Your Answer _____

Q–596

AUTOPSY
[ˋɔtɑpsɪ] : 驗屍

Your Answer _____

Q–597

POSTMORTEM
[postˋmɔrtəm] : 驗屍

Your Answer _____

Correct Answers

A–595

v.—steal
A company official who **embezzles** money can get into very serious trouble.

A–596

n.—examination of a dead body
If a person dies under strange circumstances, it is routine for an **autopsy** to be performed.

A–597

n.—examination of a dead body
The cause of death of a person can be revealed through a **postmortem**.

Questions

Q–598

EXHUME
[ɪgˋzum][ɪgˋzjum] : 挖掘

Your Answer _____

Q–599

DEPOSITION
[ˌdɛpəˋzɪʃən] : 宣誓的證言

Your Answer _____

Q–600

PERJURY
[ˋpɝdʒərɪ] : 作偽證

Your Answer _____

Correct Answers

A–598

v.—dig up
It is rare for a court to order a body to be **exhumed**.

A–599

n.—statement under oath
The expert witness gave a **deposition** in court.

A–600

n.—false statement under oath
Perjury is a serious crime because witnesses are
expected to tell the truth.

Questions

Q–601

EQUITABLE
[ˋɛkwɪtəbḷ] : 公平的

Your Answer _____

_____

Q–602

FORCIBLE
[ˋforsəbḷ] : 強制的

Your Answer _____

_____

Q–603

INDICTMENT
[ɪnˈdaɪtmənt] : 起訴

Your Answer _____

_____

Correct Answers

A–601

a.—fair

Sometimes two people in a disagreement will try to make an **equitable** arrangement before they take their argument to a court of law.

A–602

a.—aggressive

Usually the police need a search warrant from a judge before they can make a **forcible** entry into the home of a suspect.

A–603

n.—accusation

A government official suspected of wrongdoing might leave office to escape **indictment**.

Questions

Q–604

ADHERE
[əd`hɪr] : 堅持固守著

Your Answer _____

_____

Q–605

ABSTAIN
[əb`sten] : 選擇不投票

Your Answer _____

_____

Q–606

QUELL
[kwɛl] : 鎮壓

Your Answer _____

_____

Correct Answers

A–604

v.—stick

Some justices **adhere** to a conservative interpretation of the Constitution, while others are more liberal.

A–605

v.—sit out, refrain

A Supreme Court judge does not have to vote on every single case because he or she can **abstain** from voting.

A–606

v.—quench, put down

Many people do not know that President George Washington **quelled** a popular uprising that was later known as the Whiskey Rebellion.

Questions

Q–607

AUTOCRATIC
[ˌɔtə`krætɪk] : 獨裁的

Your Answer _____

_____

Q–608

RETRIBUTION
[ˌrɛtrə`bjuʃən] : 報復

Your Answer _____

_____

Q–609

COGENT
[`kodʒənt] : 有説服力的

Your Answer _____

_____

Correct Answers

A–607

a.—dictatorial
People who disliked the **autocratic** ways of President
Andrew Jackson called him King Andrew the First.

A–608

n.—revenge
During the American Civil War, the Northern forces
turned General Robert E. Lee's home into a graveyard
as **retribution** for his joining the Southern side.

A–609

a.—persuasive
President Lincoln made **cogent** arguments against
slavery.

Questions

Q–610

PROCLAIM
[prə`klem] : 宣告

Your Answer _____

Q–611

EMANCIPATE
[ɪ`mænsə‚pet] : 解放

Your Answer _____

Q–612

STIPULATE
[`stɪpjə‚let] : 規定

Your Answer _____

Correct Answers

A–610

v.—announce
During the Civil War, President Lincoln signed an
order that **proclaimed** slaves in the Southern states to
be free.

A–611

v.—make free
Many historians think that England and France kept
out of the Civil War because Lincoln **emancipated**
the slaves.

A–612

v.—specify
The law **stipulates** that slavery is illegal.

Questions

Q–613

COMPULSION
[kəm`pʌlʃən] : 強迫

Your Answer _____

_____

Q–614

TANTAMOUNT
[`tæntə‚maʊnt] : 相當於

Your Answer _____

_____

Q–615

TRUSTWORTHY
[`trʌst‚wɜðɪ] : 可信賴的

Your Answer _____

_____

Correct Answers

A–613

n.—using force to make someone do something
After the Civil War ended, Union troops used
compulsion against former slaveholders who did not
want freed slaves to exercise their rights.

A–614

a.—equivalent
In the early twentieth century, some politicians were
openly racist, a position that would be **tantamount** to
political suicide today.

A–615

a.—credible
As the Vietnam War progressed, fewer and fewer
Americans believed that President Lyndon Johnson
made **trustworthy** statements about the conflict.

Questions

Q–616

BOG
[bɑg] : 使陷入

Your Answer _____

Q–617

FRUITION
[fru`ɪʃən] : 實現

Your Answer _____

Q–618

ERUDITE
[`ɛrʊˌdaɪt] : 博學的

Your Answer _____

Correct Answers

A–616

v.—get stuck
American generals thought they would have an easy
victory, but their troops soon were **bogged** down in
the Vietnam conflict.

A–617

n.—realization
President Lyndon Johnson's plans to get re-elected
never came to **fruition**.

A–618

a.—learned
Woodrow Wilson, the only president to have a
doctoral degree, was one of America's most **erudite**
leaders.

Questions

Q–619

EXUDE
[ɪg`zud] [ɛk`sud]: 展現，散發出

Your Answer _____

_____

Q–620

AFFABLE
['æfəbl̩] : 平易近人的

Your Answer _____

_____

Q–621

CHUM
[tʃʌm] : 好友

Your Answer _____

_____

Correct Answers

A–619

v.—radiate

President Franklin Roosevelt **exuded** confidence as he led the nation.

A–620

a.—friendly

President Franklin Roosevelt had a reputation for being an **affable** politician who could charm most anyone.

A–621

n.—friend

Roosevelt and Churchill seemed to be **chums**, but their relationship was also very political.

Questions

Q–622

BANTER
['bæntə] : 聊天

Your Answer

Q–623

UNSCATHED
[ʌnˋskeðɪd] : 未受傷的

Your Answer

Q–624

RELINQUISH
[rɪˋlɪŋkwɪʃ] : 放棄

Your Answer

Correct Answers

A–622

n.—chitchat, small talk
Winston Churchill and Franklin Roosevelt would often enjoy some casual **banter** before talking about serious world issues.

A–623

a.—unhurt
President Franklin Roosevelt emerged **unscathed** from an assassination attempt.

A–624

v.—give up
President Jimmy Carter signed a document to **relinquish** control of the Panama Canal.

Questions

Q–625

SCRIBBLE
[`skrɪbḷ] : 速寫

Your Answer

Q–626

ANNEX
[ə`nɛks] : 併吞

Your Answer

Q–627

FERVENT
[`fɝvənt] : 熱切的

Your Answer

Correct Answers

A–625

v.—write quickly

Some historians say that Abraham Lincoln **scribbled** the famous Gettysburg Address on the back of an envelope.

A–626

v.—take over

President Ulysses S. Grant wanted to **annex** the nation of Santo Domingo, but he was stopped by the Senate.

A–627

a.—passionate

President Grant had the **fervent** desire to finish writing his autobiography before he died, and he accomplished his goal.

Questions

Q–628

AGONIZE
[`ægəˌnaɪz] : 痛苦掙扎

Your Answer _____

Q–629

SCOFF
[skɑf][skɔf] : 嘲笑

Your Answer _____

Q–630

FALLACIOUS
[fə`leʃəs] : 欺瞞的

Your Answer _____

419

Correct Answers

A–628

v.—struggle

President Harry Truman **agonized** over the decision to drop the atomic bomb.

A–629

v.—laugh at

Many people **scoffed** at Harry Truman when he ran for president, but he had the last laugh.

A–630

a.—deceitful

Richard Nixon made **fallacious** statements about his involvement in the Watergate scandal.

Questions

Q–631

INDIGNITY
[ɪn`dɪgnətɪ] : 不名譽

Your Answer _____

Q–632

IMPEACH
[ɪm`pitʃ] : 彈劾，指控

Your Answer _____

Q–633

CONSECUTIVE
[kən`sɛkjətɪv] : 連續的

Your Answer _____

Correct Answers

A–631

n.—dishonor

Richard Nixon resigned the presidency to escape the **indignity** of an impeachment.

A–632

v.—accuse a government official

Only two presidents in U.S. history have been **impeached**: Andrew Johnson and Bill Clinton.

A–633

a.—successive

Gerald Ford was elected to thirteen **consecutive** terms in Congress before he went to the White House.

Questions

Q–634

TUMULT
[`tjumʌlt] : 混亂

Your Answer _____

_____

Q–635

REBUKE
[rɪ`bjuk] : 指責

Your Answer _____

_____

Q–636

RETROSPECT
[`rɛtrəˌspɛkt] : 回想，回顧

Your Answer _____

_____

Correct Answers

A–634

n.—disturbance
President Ford came to office when America was in **tumult** because of the Watergate scandal.

A–635

v.—criticize
President Ford believed the Nixon pardon would heal the nation, but many people **rebuked** him for his decision at the time.

A–636

n.—hindsight
In **retrospect,** even his critics agree that President Ford's pardon of Nixon helped heal the country.

Questions

Q–637

CANDOR
[`kændə] : 坦誠

Your Answer _____

Q–638

CONDOLENCE
[kən`doləns] : 哀悼

Your Answer _____

Q–639

EULOGY
[`julədʒɪ] : 頌詞

Your Answer _____

Correct Answers

A–637

n.—frankness

President Ford was often described as a man of **candor**, dignity, and integrity.

A–638

n.—sympathy

People from all over the country expressed their **condolences** after Gerald Ford's passing.

A–639

n.—tribute

President Bush delivered the **eulogy** at former President Ford's funeral.

Questions

Q–640

PLEBEIAN
[plɪˋbiən] : 平民化的，普及的

Your Answer _____

Q–641

CALLOUS
[ˋkæləs] : 冷淡的，不在乎的

Your Answer _____

Q–642

PLACATE
[ˋpleket] : 安撫

Your Answer _____

Correct Answers

A–640

a.—popular, common

Long ago, an American had to own land before he was allowed to vote in an election, but over time, the U.S. has become more **plebeian** with regard to voting rights.

A–641

a.—cold, indifferent

It is hard for a politician to take a **callous** attitude towards the poor when the poor vote in large numbers.

A–642

v.—appease

One of the key things to understand about a democracy is that lawmakers seek to **placate** the largest number of voters.

Questions

Q–643

ELATION
[ɪˋleʃən] : 興高采烈

Your Answer _____

_____

Q–644

TALLY
[ˋtælɪ] : 計算

Your Answer _____

_____

Q–645

DESPONDENT
[dɪˋspɑndənt] : 灰心氣餒的，鬱悶的

Your Answer _____

_____

Correct Answers

A–643

n.—excitement, joy

The **elation** of winning an election soon gives way to worries about how to get re-elected.

A–644

v.—count

Electronic voting machines make it easier to **tally** votes.

A–645

a.—depressed, unhappy, gloomy

Candidates try not to become **despondent** when the polls show that their run for office is hopeless.

Questions

Q–646

DEJECTED
[dɪˋdʒɛktɪd] : 沮喪的

Your Answer _____

Q–647

CAPRICIOUS
[kəˋprɪʃəs] : 善變的

Your Answer _____

Q–648

KNACK
[næk] : 本領

Your Answer _____

Correct Answers

A–646

a.—depressed, gloomy
Politicians are **dejected** when they do not win
elections, but they need to appear as "good losers"
who are not upset.

A–647

a.—changeable
Public opinion can be **capricious**.

A–648

n.—aptitude
Some political candidates have a **knack** for
communicating with the public.

Questions

Q–649

REPEL
[rɪ`pɛl] : 擊退

Your Answer _____

Q–650

SLANDER
[`slændɚ] : 中傷，誹謗

Your Answer _____

Q–651

MALIGN
[mə`laɪn] : 惡意的

Your Answer _____

Correct Answers

A–649

v.—push back

Candidates need to have strategies to **repel** attacks from their opponents.

A–650

n.—damage

There is a fine line between negative advertising and outright **slander**.

A–651

a.—evil

When a candidate speaks negatively about his opponent, he will usually deny that he has any intention to **malign** that opponent.

Questions

Q–652

FILTHY
[ˋfɪlθɪ] : 污穢的

Your Answer _____

Q–653

ACCOUNTABILITY
[əˌkaʊntəˋbɪlətɪ] : 責任

Your Answer _____

Q–654

OFFENSIVE
[əˋfɛnsɪv] : 侮辱的

Your Answer _____

Correct Answers

A–652

a.—dirty
Candidates can lose votes if the voters think their ads
are **filthy**.

A–653

n.—responsibility
Many candidates state which ads they approve as a
way to put some **accountability** into their campaigns.

A–654

a.—insulting
Offensive language can turn away voters.

Questions

Q–655

ELICIT
[ɪˋlɪsɪt] : 引起

Your Answer _____

Q–656

CYNICAL
[ˋsɪnɪkḷ] : 懷疑消極的

Your Answer _____

Q–657

BLAST
[blæst] : 譴責抨擊

Your Answer _____

Correct Answers

A–655

v.—bring forth
Sometimes the responses to political advertisements are not what the advertisers intend to **elicit**.

A–656

a.—doubtful
Negative advertisements make some people feel **cynical** about politics.

A–657

v.—criticize
Candidates who make outrageous statements risk getting **blasted** by the media or their opponents.

Questions

Q–658

INCLINATION
[ˌɪnkləˋneʃən] : 傾向

Your Answer _____

Q–659

STRAIGHTFORWARD
[ˌstretˋfɔrwɚd] : 直接了當的

Your Answer _____

Q–660

UNEQUIVOCAL
[ˌʌnɪˋkwɪvəkḷ] : 不含糊的，非模稜兩可的

Your Answer _____

Correct Answers

A–658

n.—tendency
Many candidates have an **inclination** to be careful
with their words.

A–659

a.—direct
Candidates do not always give **straightforward**
answers during a political debate.

A–660

a.—unambiguous
Voters expect a candidate to provide **unequivocal**
statements on taxes.

Questions

Q–661

QUIBBLE
[ˋkwɪbḷ] : （避重就輕地）爭論

Your Answer _____

Q–662

SARCASM
[ˋsɑrkæzm̩] : 諷刺

Your Answer _____

Q–663

ALIENATE
[ˋeljənˌet] : 使遠離

Your Answer _____

Correct Answers

A–661

v.—argue

If candidates **quibble** too much about the exact meanings of their public statements, it might be hard to make voters trust them.

A–662

n.—bitterness

People talk with **sarcasm** about politicians who shift their positions.

A–663

v.—turn away

Candidates try not to **alienate** their supporters.

Questions

Q–664

ERR
[ɛr][ɜ] : 犯錯

Your Answer _____

Q–665

AGGRAVATE
[`ægrə͵vet] : 使越糟

Your Answer _____

Q–666

ENDORSE
[ɪn`dɔrs] : 認同支持

Your Answer _____

Correct Answers

A–664

v.—mistake

Everybody **errs** on occasion, but some politicians have difficulty admitting a mistake.

A–665

v.—worsen

Not admitting a mistake might **aggravate** a problem, not make it go away.

A–666

v.—support

It is common for organizations to **endorse** a candidate.

Questions

Q–667

DISPEL
[dɪˋspɛl] : 驅除

Your Answer _____

Q–668

MISGIVING
[mɪsˋgɪvɪŋ] : 疑慮

Your Answer _____

Q–669

APATHETIC
[ˌæpəˋθɛtɪk] : 漠不關心的

Your Answer _____

Correct Answers

A–667

v.—clear
Candidates seek to **dispel** doubts that voters may
have about them.

A–668

n.—doubt
A candidate might not win if the voters have
misgivings about his honesty.

A–669

a.—indifferent
Apathetic voters are bad for a democracy.

Questions

Q–670

WOO
[wu] : 吸引爭取

Your Answer _____

Q–671

DISSEMINATE
[dɪˋsɛməˏnet] : 宣傳散佈

Your Answer _____

Q–672

ENVISAGE
[ɪnˋvɪzɪdʒ] : 想像

Your Answer _____

Correct Answers

A–670

v.—attract, court

More and more politicians are doing their best to **woo** younger voters.

A–671

v.—spread

It is common now for politicians to **disseminate** their messages on the Internet.

A–672

v.—imagine

Many politicians **envisage** a future in the White House.

Questions

Q–673

INCUMBENT
[ɪn`kʌmbənt] : 現任職位者

Your Answer _____

Q–674

ARCHAEOLOGY
[ˌɑrkɪ`ɑlədʒɪ] : 考古學

Your Answer _____

Q–675

EXCAVATION
[ˌɛkskə`veʃən] : 挖掘

Your Answer _____

Correct Answers

A–673

n.—office holder
Incumbents can be better known when they are seeking re-election, but they do not necessarily have a better chance than their opponents have.

A–674

n.—the study of ancient objects
To a large degree, the field of **archeology** was born in the eighteenth century when people discovered buried cities such as Pompeii.

A–675

n.—dig
People usually think of archaeologists as working on **excavations** in exotic places, but they spend a lot of time patiently working in labs.

Questions

Q–676

ASTOUNDING
[əs'taʊndɪŋ] : 令人驚嘆的

Your Answer _____

Q–677

ARTIFACT
[`ɑrtɪˌfækt] : 手工製品

Your Answer _____

Q–678

SCRUPULOUS
[`skrupjələs] : 確實的，一絲不苟的

Your Answer _____

Correct Answers

A–676

a.—astonishing, amazing
The discovery of the ancient city of Troy in the
nineteenth century by Heinrich Schliemann was an
astounding archaeological find.

A–677

n.—man-made object
X-ray equipment can play an important role in
studying ancient **artifacts**.

A–678

a.—accurate, careful
Archaeologists keep **scrupulous** records of a dig
since the context in which an item is found can be just
as important as the object itself.

Questions

Q–679

BRITTLE
[`brɪtḷ] : 易損壞的

Your Answer _____

Q–680

LOOT
[lut] : 搶劫

Your Answer _____

Q–681

PILLAGE
[`pɪlɪdʒ] : 掠奪

Your Answer _____

Correct Answers

A–679

a.—fragile

Many ancient objects are **brittle** and must be handled with great care.

A–680

v.—steal, rob

People sometimes **loot** antiquities from museums, especially during a war.

A–681

v.—strip, rob

Some worry that dishonest people will **pillage** archaeological sites in Iraq.

Questions

Q–682

RAMPANT
[ˋræmpənt] : 猖獗的

Your Answer _____

Q–683

LUCRATIVE
[ˋlukrətɪv] : 有利可圖的

Your Answer _____

Q–684

VIGILANCE
[ˋvɪdʒələns] : 警覺

Your Answer _____

Correct Answers

A–682

a.—widespread
Illegal digging of antiquities is **rampant** throughout the world.

A–683

a.—profitable
The $1.5 million that Moshe Dayan's widow received for his collection of antiquities shows how **lucrative** digging can be.

A–684

n.—alertness, attention
It takes **vigilance** to prevent archaeological sites from being robbed.

Questions

Q–685

DISTRAUGHT
[dɪˋstrɔt] : 煩躁難過的，忐忑不安的

Your Answer _____

_____

Q–686

LETHARGIC
[lɪˋθɑrdʒɪk] : 懶洋洋的，倦怠的

Your Answer _____

_____

Q–687

INSTIGATE
[ˋɪnstəˏget] : 鼓動

Your Answer _____

_____

Correct Answers

A–685

a.—upset

Children nowadays might be **distraught** on the first day of school, but 100 years ago many children had to work in mines and factories.

A–686

a.—lazy

A snack that is high in sugar gives children energy, but a few hours later they become **lethargic**.

A–687

v.—cause

Sometimes there is one young troublemaker who **instigates** much of the bad behavior in a classroom.

Questions

Q–688

TENUOUS
[ˋtɛnjʊəs] : 薄弱的

Your Answer _____

Q–689

SCUFFLE
[ˋskʌfḷ] : 打鬥

Your Answer _____

Q–690

PRECOCIOUS
[prɪˋkoʃəs] : 早熟的

Your Answer _____

Correct Answers

A–688

a.—weak

Some people believe that violent video games are dangerous for a troubled child who already has a **tenuous** hold on reality.

A–689

n.—fight

A teacher should try to break up a **scuffle** between two young students.

A–690

a.—advanced

A **precocious** child might need more intellectual challenges and freedom.

Questions

Q–691

AGILITY
[ə`dʒɪlətɪ] : 靈活，敏捷

Your Answer _____

Q–692

BADGER
[`bædʒɚ] : 纏著，糾纏

Your Answer _____

Q–693

GRATIFY
[`grætəˌfaɪ] : 滿足

Your Answer _____

Correct Answers

A–691

n.—flexibility

Play outdoors and physical exercise help children to develop strength and **agility**.

A–692

v.—nag

Some children **badger** their parents to buy them popular toys and clothes.

A–693

v.—satisfy

Parents can spoil children if they **gratify** their every desire.

Questions

Q–694

EMBITTER
[ɪmˋbɪtə] : 使埋怨

Your Answer _____

_____

Q–695

FICTITIOUS
[fɪkˋtɪʃəs] : 虛構的

Your Answer _____

_____

Q–696

SEQUEL
[ˋsikwəl] : 續集

Your Answer _____

_____

Correct Answers

A–694

v.—make resentful
Children can become **embittered** if their elders break promises.

A–695

a.—made-up
Many children have fallen in love with the **fictitious** character of Harry Potter.

A–696

n.—follow-up
The readers were anxiously waiting for a Harry Potter **sequel**.

Questions

Q–697

DISSENSION
[dɪˋsɛnʃən] : 意見不合

Your Answer _____

Q–698

ARDOR
[ˋɑrdə] : 熱忱

Your Answer _____

Q–699

BEDECK
[bɪˋdɛk] : 裝飾

Your Answer _____

Correct Answers

A–697

n.—disagreement
Dissension in the ranks of a conservative society can be dangerous.

A–698

n.—passion
Some people have **ardor** for community service, but others don't care.

A–699

v.—decorate
Communist countries would often **bedeck** their buildings with large banners that were supposed to inspire the people.

Questions

Q–700

BUTT
[bʌt]：目標，（嘲笑的）對象

Your Answer _____

_____

Q–701

DEVIATE
[ˋdivɪˌet]：偏離

Your Answer _____

_____

Q–702

HAGGLE
[ˋhægḷ]：議價，討價還價

Your Answer _____

_____

Correct Answers

A–700

n.—target
When the leaders of a community become the **butt** of jokes, you can guess that something is wrong.

A–701

v.—depart
A person who **deviates** from basic rules of good behavior can have a bad effect on his neighborhood.

A–702

v.—bargain
In some cultures, it is okay to **haggle** over prices at the market.

Questions

Q–703

REBATE
[`ribet] : 退款回饋

Your Answer _____

Q–704

EXPEDITIOUS
[ˌɛkspɪ`dɪʃəs] : 迅速的

Your Answer _____

Q–705

DISPATCH
[dɪ`spætʃ] : 派遣

Your Answer _____

Correct Answers

A–703

n.—partial repayment
Some manufacturers try to increase sales of their products by offering **rebates**.

A–704

a.—prompt
A technology company needs to know what its competition is doing and plan an **expeditious** response.

A–705

v.—send
In ancient times, a way to communicate was to **dispatch** a horse rider bearing a message.

Questions

Q–706

LACONIC
[lə`kɑnɪk] : 簡略的

Your Answer _____

Q–707

HEYDAY
[`hede] : 全盛期

Your Answer _____

Q–708

ANACHRONISM
[ə`nækrə‚nɪzəm] : 過時，不合潮流

Your Answer _____

Correct Answers

A–706

a.—brief
Julius Caesar sent a **laconic** three-word letter to the Roman Senate.

A–707

n.—best days
In their **heyday**, sailing ships carried most international trade and communications.

A–708

n.—something out of date
Some people think that a hand-written letter is an **anachronism** in the age of email.

Questions

Q–709

BONA FIDE
[`bonə`faɪdɪ] : 真實的

Your Answer _____

_____

Q–710

BIBLIOPHILE
[`bɪblɪəˌfaɪl] : 愛書的人

Your Answer _____

_____

Q–711

DICTUM
[`dɪktəm] : 名言

Your Answer _____

_____

Correct Answers

A–709

a.—genuine, authentic

An expert can tell if a paper document is **bona fide**, but it can be harder to detect a fake email.

A–710

n.—book lover

Nowadays, **bibliophiles** have a much easier time adding to their libraries since they can purchase books online.

A–711

n.—motto

It is a famous **dictum** of communication that "the medium is the message."

Q–712

PANACEA
[ˌpænəˈsiə] : 萬能丹

Your Answer

Q–713

INSATIABLE
[ɪnˈseʃɪəbl] : 永不滿足的

Your Answer

Q–714

SATURATE
[ˈsætʃəˌret] : 浸透；飽和

Your Answer

Correct Answers

A–712

n.—cure-all

One hundred years ago, better communication was a **panacea**, but today we often think that it is part of the problem.

A–713

a.—cannot be satisfied

Some argue that people have an **insatiable** appetite for news.

A–714

v.—soak

Today we are **saturated** with so much information and so many kinds of entertainment that it can be hard to find what we really like.

Questions

Q–715

INVECTIVE
[ɪn`vɛktɪv] : 惡言謾罵

Your Answer _____

Q–716

RADICAL
[`rædɪkl̩] : 極端的

Your Answer _____

Q–717

SLIT
[slɪt] : 切開

Your Answer _____

Correct Answers

A–715

n.—scolding

When people look at some news shows, they often ask themselves if they are watching journalism or political **invective**.

A–716

a.—extreme

Throwing away all of your mail is a **radical** solution to the problem of junk mail.

A–717

v.—cut

Some people use a special tool to **slit** envelopes.

Questions

Q–718

CLANDESTINE
[klæn`dɛstɪn] : 秘密的

Your Answer

Q–719

GERMINATE
[`dʒɝməˌnet] : 成形，產生

Your Answer

Q–720

AUDACIOUS
[ɔ`deʃəs] : 大膽的，無畏的

Your Answer

Correct Answers

A–718

a.—secret

Government organizations that engage in **clandestine** operations often monitor their enemies' communications.

A–719

v.—sprout, emerge

The computer is an idea that took a long time to **germinate**.

A–720

a.—bold

In the 1980s, Osborne was the first company to do something that was **audacious** for the time: make a computer that had a built-in screen.

Questions

Q–721

EXTOL
[ɪk`stol] : 讚揚

Your Answer _____

Q–722

LUG
[lʌg] : 拖拉

Your Answer _____

Q–723

ACQUIRE
[ə`kwaɪr] : 取得

Your Answer _____

Correct Answers

A–721

v.—praise

The first personal computers were **extolled** as tools for learning, but many people nowadays buy computers for entertainment.

A–722

v.—carry

Before laptops were invented, it was a big thing to own a personal computer that you could **lug** around.

A–723

v.—get

When someone **acquires** a computer, usually the first thing he or she wants to do is to look at the World Wide Web.

Questions

Q–724

ENCOMPASS
[ɪn`kʌmpəs] : 包含

Your Answer _____

_____

Q–725

ARRAY
[ə`re] : 一系列

Your Answer _____

_____

Q–726

SYNCHRONIZE
[`sɪŋkrə͵naɪz] : 使同步，使一致

Your Answer _____

_____

Correct Answers

A–724

v.—include

Nowadays, the World Wide Web really does **encompass** almost the entire world.

A–725

n.—range

Computers allow users to do an **array** of tasks at the same time.

A–726

v.—match, coordinate

You can automatically **synchronize** your computer's clock with a timeserver.

Questions

Q–727

LOAFER
[ˋlofɚ] : 遊手好閒的人

Your Answer _____

_____

Q–728

SPORADIC
[spoˋrædɪk] : 偶發的

Your Answer _____

_____

Q–729

ADEQUATE
[ˋædəkwɪt] : 足夠的

Your Answer _____

_____

Correct Answers

A–727

n.—idler
Loafers used to sit around all day watching television, but now many of them cruise the World Wide Web.

A–728

a.—random, irregular
Sporadic computer problems can be hard to figure out.

A–729

a.—enough
Consumers need to know that Internet shopping sites have **adequate** security.

Questions

Q–730

INTERMITTENT
[͵ɪntə`mɪtṇt] : 時斷時續的

Your Answer _____

Q–731

ACRID
[`ækrɪd] : 辛辣的

Your Answer _____

Q–732

CIRCUMSCRIBE
[`sɝkəm͵skraɪb] : 限制

Your Answer _____

Correct Answers

A–730

a.—occasional

Intermittent problems with computer software or hardware can be the most difficult to fix.

A–731

a.—sharp

If you smell the **acrid** odor of burning plastic, you should shut off your computer.

A–732

v.—limit

Some people **circumscribe** their computer use when they find out how dangerous the Internet is.

Questions

Q–733

RIFE
[raɪf] : 非常多的

Your Answer _____

Q–734

FORGE
[fɔrdʒ] : 偽造

Your Answer _____

Q–735

CONGREGATE
[`kɑŋgrɪˌget] : 聚集

Your Answer _____

Correct Answers

A–733

a.—overflowing

The Internet is **rife** with traps.

A–734

v.—fake

The Internet seems to make it easier for thieves since they don't need to **forge** a signature.

A–735

v.—gather

Some Web sites have a forum area where they expect people to **congregate** and discuss matters.

Questions

Q–736

PROVISION
[prə`vɪʒən] : 條款規定

Your Answer _____

Q–737

UNSOLICITED
[ˌʌnsə`lɪsɪtɪd] : 未經索取的

Your Answer _____

Q–738

LASH
[læʃ] : 抨擊

Your Answer _____

Correct Answers

A–736

n.—condition
The **provisions** of an agreement are often in small print, and some people simply ignore them.

A–737

a.—unrequested
Many people receive **unsolicited** email every day.

A–738

v.—strike
It is impossible to **lash** out at all the people who send us junk email because there are too many of them.

Questions

Q–739

DELUGE
[`dɛljudʒ] : 氾濫

Your Answer _____

Q–740

INTRUSION
[ɪn`truʒən] : 入侵

Your Answer _____

Q–741

APPROPRIATE
[ə`proprɪet] : 適當的

Your Answer _____

Correct Answers

A–739

n.—flood
Today we face a daily **deluge** of junk mail and junk email.

A–740

n.—invasion
Computer users feel secure if their computer systems are capable of detecting attempts at **intrusion**.

A–741

a.—proper
Government lawmakers have tried to take the **appropriate** steps to make the Internet safe.

Questions

Q–742

HARASS
[hə`ræs][`hærəs] : 騷擾

Your Answer _____

Q–743

DISCONCERT
[ˌdɪskən`sɝt] : 使慌張，使擔憂

Your Answer _____

Q–744

ADMINISTER
[əd`mɪnəstə] : 掌管

Your Answer _____

Correct Answers

A–742

v.—bother
In some countries, it is a crime to **harass** someone
through email.

A–743

v.—worry
Knowing the damage hackers can do **disconcerts**
many computer users.

A–744

v.—control
The people who **administer** computer networks are
highly trained, and so are hackers.

Questions

Q–745

BREACH

[britʃ] : 漏洞，缺裂

Your Answer _____

Q–746

DELUDE

[dɪˋlud] : 欺騙

Your Answer _____

Q–747

FRAUD

[ˋfrɔd] : 騙局

Your Answer _____

Correct Answers

A–745

n.—break

An administrator should be able to recognize a potential **breach** of security of the system.

A–746

v.—deceive

When Web-based commerce began, some people were **deluded** into thinking that all their transactions were safe.

A–747

n.—deceit

Internet **fraud** is a serious problem.

Questions

Q–748

INDEMNIFY
[ɪnˋdɛmnəˌfaɪ] : 賠償

Your Answer _____

_____

Q–749

INCUR
[ɪnˋkɝ] : 使自身遭受

Your Answer _____

_____

Q–750

FEIGN
[fen] : 假裝

Your Answer _____

_____

Correct Answers

A–748

v.—repay
Account holders are asked to **indemnify** losses that are caused by the users themselves.

A–749

v.—bring upon oneself
Banks usually cover losses that an account holder might **incur** when a credit card holder is a victim of theft.

A–750

v.—pretend
Banks certainly will not allow customers to **feign** ignorance of the rules.

Questions

Q–751

CONSOLIDATE
[kən`sɑləˌdet] : 整合，統一

Your Answer _____

_____

Q–752

MANEUVER
[mə`nuvə] : 策動；策略

Your Answer _____

_____

Q–753

STUPENDOUS
[stu`pɛndəs] : 巨大的

Your Answer _____

_____

Correct Answers

A–751

v.—combine, unite
Some people keep balances on several credit cards, but others **consolidate** their debt into one bill.

A–752

n.—move
In 1651, in a clever **maneuver**, the British banned Dutch ships from transporting goods to English colonies so that their own shippers would have a monopoly.

A–753

a.—huge
Although Britain had a **stupendous** empire, it was the low wages paid to English factory workers that made British products sell well around the world.

Questions

Q–754

SUBSIDY
[`sʌbsədɪ] : 補助金

Your Answer _____

_____

Q–755

OUTSPOKEN
[aʊt`spokən] : 坦率直言的

Your Answer _____

_____

Q–756

COLLUSION
[kə`luʒən] : 共謀

Your Answer _____

_____

Correct Answers

A–754

n.—financial aid

In the eighteenth century, the English used **subsidies** to build up their cotton textile industry.

A–755

a.—frank

Leo Amery was a British politician who was an **outspoken** critic of free trade after the Second World War.

A–756

n.—conspiracy

It was not **collusion** but rather a series of accidents that caused many countries to stop using silver money in the late nineteenth century.

Questions

Q–757

COMPENSATION
[ˌkampənˋseʃən] : 賠償

Your Answer _____

_____

Q–758

INORDINATE
[ɪnˋɔrdn̩ɪt] : 過度的

Your Answer _____

_____

Q–759

PECUNIARY
[pɪˋkjunɪˌɛrɪ] : 財務方面的

Your Answer _____

_____

Correct Answers

A–757

n.—payment
When the German Empire received a large amount of gold from the French in 1873 as **compensation** for the Franco-Prussian War, Germany stopped using silver money.

A–758

a.—extreme
Other countries followed the German lead, and this caused an economic depression and an **inordinate** amount of suffering.

A–759

a.—financial
Knowing that American farmers had **pecuniary** difficulties when silver money was withdrawn, William Jennings Bryan gave a famous "Cross of Gold" speech against the move away from silver.

Questions

Q–760

CONTIGUOUS
[kən`tɪgjʊəs] : 鄰近的

Your Answer _____

Q–761

STRIFE
[straɪf] : 衝突，不和

Your Answer _____

Q–762

INDIGENOUS
[ɪn`dɪdʒənəs] : 本地的

Your Answer _____

Correct Answers

A–760

a.—adjacent

In today's world, people do not limit their business partners to **contiguous** countries.

A–761

n.—disagreement

There has always been **strife** between people who want free trade and those who want to protect national industries.

A–762

a.—native

Many Western governments no longer try to protect their **indigenous** workforce but allow jobs to be moved out of the country.

Questions

Q–763

AGGREGATE
[ˋægrɪˏget] : 總計

Your Answer _____

Q–764

SUFFICE
[səˋfaɪs] : 足夠

Your Answer _____

Q–765

ALBEIT
[əlˋbiɪt] : 雖然

Your Answer _____

Correct Answers

A–763

n.—combination
The Gross National Product (GNP) is an **aggregate** number that is composed of statistics from many industries.

A–764

v.—be enough
The Gross National Product does not **suffice** to tell everything that is happening in the economy.

A–765

conj.—although
Some economists and officials complain about the limitations of the Gross National Product **albeit** it makes big economic trends easier to understand.

Questions

Q–766

APPALL
[ə`pɔl] : 驚訝

Your Answer _____

Q–767

OFFSET
[`ɔf,sɛt] : 彌補，抵銷

Your Answer _____

Q–768

OBVIATE
[`ɑbvɪ,et] : 除去

Your Answer _____

Correct Answers

A–766

v.—shock
Some people are **appalled** to find out that governments sometimes pay farmers not to grow crops, but it is a way to keep prices up.

A–767

v.—counterbalance
Some government payments are used to **offset** losses when agricultural prices drop.

A–768

v.—remove
Credit cards and bank cards **obviate** the need to carry large amounts of cash.

Questions

Q–769

DOGMATIC
[dɔg`mætɪk] : 獨斷的

Your Answer

Q–770

PRECONCEPTION
[ˌprikən`sɛpʃən] : 先入之見

Your Answer

Q–771

SPREE
[spri] : 縱容，瘋狂（採購）

Your Answer

Correct Answers

A–769

a.—rigid, doctrinaire

In the early part of the twentieth century, economists were more **dogmatic** while today many are more flexible.

A–770

n.—assumption

The increasing pace of technological and social change has shattered many of our **preconceptions** about economics.

A–771

n.—wild outing

Some policy makers encourage spending **sprees** to stimulate the economy.

Questions

Q–772

FRUGAL
[`frugl] : 節儉的

Your Answer _____

Q–773

ASTUTE
[ə`stjut] : 精明的

Your Answer _____

Q–774

LEVERAGE
[`lɛvərɪdʒ] : 勢力

Your Answer _____

Correct Answers

A–772

a.—economical, thrifty
Frugal shoppers care about saving and watch their
money carefully.

A–773

a.—clever
Warren Buffett is an **astute** businessman who became
one of the richest people in the world through careful
investing.

A–774

n.—power
Small special interest groups might not have the
leverage to influence politicians on a national level.

Questions

Q–775

PRECARIOUS
[prɪˋkɛrɪəs] : 不安定的

Your Answer _____

Q–776

SEASONED
[ˋsiznd] : 有經驗的

Your Answer _____

Q–777

OVERHAUL
[͵ovɚˋhɔl] : 重整

Your Answer _____

Correct Answers

A–775

a.—unstable

Some companies see new leadership as a way out of **precarious** situations.

A–776

a.—experienced, veteran

Most businesses prefer hiring a **seasoned** leader with a successful track record.

A–777

v.—reorganize

An experienced executive is expected to **overhaul** the organization of a company that is in trouble.

Questions

Q–778

FLUCTUATE
[`flʌktʃʊˌet] : 波動

Your Answer _____

Q–779

SCURRY
[`skɝɪ] : 匆促

Your Answer _____

Q–780

MUTABLE
[`mjutəbḷ] : 多變的

Your Answer _____

Correct Answers

A–778

v.—vary; waver

Everybody knows that the stock market **fluctuates**, but not all people agree as to why this is so.

A–779

v.—hurry

A negative report from the Federal Reserve Bank can cause investors to **scurry** to sell their stock.

A–780

a.—changeable

In the **mutable** world of the stock market, fortunes can be made and lost overnight.

Questions

Q–781

CRAZE
[krez] : 狂熱，一陣流行風潮

Your Answer _____

Q–782

UPSURGE
[ʌpˋsɝdʒ] : 高漲

Your Answer _____

Q–783

SPATE
[spet] : 泉湧而至

Your Answer _____

Correct Answers

A–781

n.—rage, fad

From the end of 2005 to 2006, there was a gold **craze**, and the price of gold hit a record high.

A–782

n.—increase

Gold sellers were happy to see the **upsurge** in gold prices.

A–783

n.—surge, outpouring

Not everyone thinks much of the recent **spate** of news about gold prices.

Questions

Q–784

TAPER
[`tepə] : 逐漸減少

Your Answer _____

Q–785

GLUT
[glʌt] : 供應過多

Your Answer _____

Q–786

APPAREL
[ə`pærəl] : 服裝

Your Answer _____

Correct Answers

A–784

v.—decrease gradually
The gold fever seems to have **tapered** off.

A–785

n.—excess
A **glut** of oil on the international market can lower the price of gasoline in the U.S.

A–786

n.—clothing
Textiles and **apparel** are often very important industries for developing nations.

Questions

Q–787

ABROGATE
[`æbrə͵get] : 取消

Your Answer _____

Q–788

PERPLEXING
[pə`plɛksɪŋ] : 複雜的

Your Answer _____

Q–789

NETTLE
[`nɛtḷ] : 使憤怒

Your Answer _____

Correct Answers

A–787

v.—cancel

A treaty to limit the buildup of weapons might be **abrogated** by a country that thinks the other countries are cheating.

A–788

a.—complex

Due to globalization, nations and individuals have many opportunities and also face a number of **perplexing** problems.

A–789

v.—irritate

Some people are **nettled** by the fact that jobs move to countries that have lower wages.

Questions

Q–790

CAPTIVATE
[`kæptə‚vet] : 使著迷

Your Answer

Q–791

ENTAIL
[ɪn`tel] : 伴隨

Your Answer

Q–792

CENSOR
[`sɛnsə] : （政府單位對媒體等）審查

Your Answer

Correct Answers

A–790

v.—fascinate

Eighty years ago, the first "talking films" **captivated** people, but today we take them for granted.

A–791

v.—require

Most of us do not know all the work that is **entailed** in getting a movie idea from the script to the screen.

A–792

v.—restrict

Some countries **censor** movies to make sure they do not offend political or moral standards.

Questions

Q–793

CONDONE
[kən`don] : 寬恕

Your Answer _____

_____

Q–794

FULMINATE
[`fʌlmə͵net] : 嚴詞譴責

Your Answer _____

_____

Q–795

PESTER
[`pɛstɚ] : 使煩擾

Your Answer _____

_____

Correct Answers

A–793

v.—overlook

The American government does not **condone** violence in films but allows it as part of the freedom of speech.

A–794

v.—condemn

Although the government might not order a movie to be removed from a theater, sometimes viewers **fulminate** against certain films.

A–795

v.—annoy

Some people enjoy watching violent films, but others are **pestered** by attempts to use special effects and fights to cover up the lack of a good story.

Questions

Q–796

MANDATE
[`mændet] : 權威

Your Answer _____

_____

Q–797

DIGNIFY
[`dɪgnəˌfaɪ] : 尊重

Your Answer _____

_____

Q–798

ELUDE
[ɪˋlud] : 避開

Your Answer _____

_____

Correct Answers

A–796

n.—authority
The Motion Picture Association of America,
composed of some private companies, has the
mandate to rate films.

A–797

v.—honor
If somebody asks you an insulting question, you
might decide not to **dignify** it with an answer.

A–798

v.—avoid
If success **eludes** you, keep on working hard anyway.

Questions

Q–799

GRIP
[grɪp] : 掌握，了解

Your Answer ____

Q–800

REITERATE
[riˋɪtəˏret] : 重述

Your Answer ____

Q–801

SQUANDER
[ˋskwɑndɚ] : 浪費

Your Answer ____

Correct Answers

A–799

n.—understanding
People who do not have a good **grip** on reality are
likely to run into problems.

A–800

v.—repeat
Many people trying halfheartedly to overcome a
weakness **reiterate** the prayer of a witty Frenchman:
"Oh, Lord. Make me good, but not today!"

A–801

v.—waste
If you **squander** your money, you might not have
enough when you really need it for something
important.

Questions

Q–802

GARRULOUS
[`gærələs] : 饒舌的

Your Answer _____

Q–803

LAUD
[lɔd] : 讚美

Your Answer _____

Q–804

PLY
[plaɪ] : 提供

Your Answer _____

Correct Answers

A–802

a.—talkative

Very often, **garrulous** people enjoy talking more than the members of their audience enjoy listening.

A–803

v.—praise

The Roman emperor Diocletian is one of the two people in history to be **lauded** for giving up absolute power and retiring.

A–804

v.—supply

In England at the beginning of the twentieth century, it was against the law for a politician to **ply** a voter with food and drink.

Questions

Q–805

DEFAULT
[dɪˋfɔlt] : 未履行

Your Answer

Q–806

CABAL
[kəˋbæl][kəˋbɑl] : 群黨

Your Answer

Q–807

WHEREBY
[hwɛrˋbaɪ] : 藉以

Your Answer

Correct Answers

A–805

v.—fail

A nation can run into huge financial problems if it **defaults** on its loan payments.

A–806

n.—group

In countries with weak democratic institutions, it can be easy for a **cabal** of army officers and officials to seize control of the government.

A–807

conj.—by which

Many people believe that a strong democracy is the only means **whereby** the rights of individuals can be protected.

Questions

Q–808

EVASION
[ɪˋveʒən] : 避免

Your Answer _____

_____

Q–809

HATCHET
[ˋhætʃɪt] : 小斧頭

Your Answer _____

_____

Q–810

IDEOLOGY
[ˌaɪdɪˋɑlədʒɪ] : 思想意識

Your Answer _____

_____

Correct Answers

A–808

n.—avoidance

Evasion of the issues that people fight about can help a politician keep from making enemies, but this will not win him many friends either.

A–809

n.—small ax

Sometimes a reporter will call a bad attack on somebody's reputation a **hatchet** job.

A–810

n.—doctrine

In many corners of the globe, government leaders are slowly learning to separate economic policy from political **ideology**.

Questions

Q–811

ANTIQUITY
[æn`tɪkwətɪ] : 古代

Your Answer _____

_____

Q–812

EXTINCT
[ɪk`stɪŋkt] : 已不存在的

Your Answer _____

_____

Q–813

AUGMENT
[ɔg`mɛnt] : 擴充，增加

Your Answer _____

_____

Correct Answers

A–811

n.—ancient times
Some old-fashioned romantics hold to the view
that languages were purer and better in the days of
antiquity.

A–812

a.—dead
Scholars work carefully to figure out the meaning of
ancient documents written in **extinct** languages.

A–813

v.—increase
Very often, speakers of a language will **augment**
their vocabulary by borrowing words from another
language.

Questions

Q–814

ATTRIBUTE
[ˋætrəˌbjʊt] : 屬性，特質

Your Answer _____

_____

Q–815

ARBITER
[ˋɑrbɪtɚ] : 裁決者

Your Answer _____

_____

Q–816

DISPARATE
[ˋdɪspərɪt] [dɪˋspærɪt]: 不同的

Your Answer _____

_____

Correct Answers

A–814
n.—feature

In Latin, nouns can be masculine, feminine, or neuter, but many languages do not have these **attributes** built into their grammar.

A–815
n.—judge

A literary critic is often more an **arbiter** of good taste than a guardian of the language.

A–816
a.—different

Historical linguists maintain that **disparate** languages such as French, Swedish, and Bulgarian have a common ancestor.

Questions

Q–817

DISPARITY
[dɪsˋpærətɪ] : 不同

Your Answer _____

Q–818

DYNAMIC
[daɪˋnæmɪk] : 有動力的

Your Answer _____

Q–819

GABBLING
[ˋgæblɪŋ] : 無意義的聲音

Your Answer _____

Correct Answers

A–817

n.—difference

A **disparity** between the way something is spelled and the way it is pronounced can be a sign that the language has changed.

A–818

a.—active

Linguists say that languages are **dynamic** and constantly changing.

A–819

n.—nonsense

When you hear people speak a language you do not know, it might sound like **gabbling**.

Questions

Q–820

ERRONEOUS
[ɪˋronɪəs] : 錯誤的

Your Answer _____

Q–821

RAZE
[rez] : 毀壞

Your Answer _____

Q–822

DIMINUTIVE
[dəˋmɪnjətɪv]: 小型的

Your Answer _____

Correct Answers

A–820

a.—wrong

Long ago, many people held the **erroneous** belief that the world was flat.

A–821

v.—destroy

Barbarians **razed** the city of Rome several times, and these misfortunes sped up the fall of the Roman Empire.

A–822

a.—small

People in the Middle Ages were more **diminutive** than we are today since they did not eat as well as we do.

Questions

Q–823

PROFANE
[prə`fen] : 不敬的，有瀆神明的

Your Answer _____

_____

Q–824

PROSCRIBED
[pro`skraɪbd] : 禁止的

Your Answer _____

_____

Q–825

PROTRACTED
[pro`træktɪd] : 長期拖延的

Your Answer _____

_____

Correct Answers

A–823

a.—unholy

People in the Middle Ages paid serious attention to the distinction between the sacred and the **profane**.

A–824

a.—forbidden

In the Middle Ages in western Europe, there was a list of **proscribed** books that people were not allowed to read.

A–825

a.—prolonged

The Hundred Years' War was a **protracted** conflict between England and France.

Questions

Q–826

CONTEMPTUOUS
[kən`tɛmptʃʊəs] : 蔑視的

Your Answer _____

Q–827

DAUNTLESS
[`dɔntlɪs] : 大膽無畏的

Your Answer _____

Q–828

IMPREGNABLE
[ɪm`prɛgnəbḷ] : 攻不破的

Your Answer _____

Correct Answers

A–826

a.—looking down upon, scornful

At that time, nobles were **contemptuous** of the growing middle class.

A–827

a.—fearless

The **dauntless** Ferdinand Magellan was the first explorer to sail around the world.

A–828

a.—unconquerable

The walls of Constantinople had been **impregnable** for more than a thousand years, but they fell in 1453.

Questions

Q–829

OPULENCE
[`ɑpjələns] : 財富

Your Answer _____

Q–830

MONARCHY
[`mɑnəkɪ] : 君主國

Your Answer _____

Q–831

UNDERSCORE
[ˌʌndə`skor] : 強調

Your Answer _____

Correct Answers

A–829

n.—wealth

The **opulence** of royal palaces was to convince people of the strength and importance of the nation and the king.

A–830

n.—government by a king

Machiavelli (1469-1527), an Italian political philosopher, believed that a strong **monarchy** would be the way to achieve peace in society.

A–831

v.—emphasize

Machiavelli's book *The Prince* **underscores** the importance of a leader being strong and clever.

Questions

Q–832

EXEMPLARY
[ɪgˋzɛmplərɪ] : 值得仿效的

Your Answer _____

Q–833

DEFERENCE
[ˋdɛfərəns] : 尊敬服從

Your Answer _____

Q–834

INCARCERATE
[ɪnˋkɑrsə͵ret] : 拘禁，關進監牢

Your Answer _____

Correct Answers

A–832

a.—worthy of imitation

His book is considered an **exemplary** study of political power.

A–833

n.—respect

He believed that rulers must be treated with **deference**.

A–834

v.—imprison

Because of a political plot, Machiavelli was **incarcerated** for a while.

Questions

Q–835

DUNGEON
[`dʌndʒən] : 地牢

Your Answer _____

Q–836

CANDID
[`kændɪd] : 坦白

Your Answer _____

Q–837

PROMULGATE
[prə`mʌɫget] : 宣導

Your Answer _____

Correct Answers

A–835

n.—underground prison
He was confined in a **dungeon**.

A–836

a.—frank
Machiavelli was **candid** in describing what worked in the cold, hard world of political reality.

A–837

v.—promote
Napoleon **promulgated** French ideas of liberty and progress throughout the lands he conquered.

Questions

Q–838

QUASH
[kwɑʃ] : 鎮壓

Your Answer _____

_____

Q–839

IMPETUOUS
[ɪmˋpɛtʃʊəs] : 輕率的

Your Answer _____

_____

Q–840

BELLIGERENT
[bəˋlɪdʒərənt] : 交戰國

Your Answer _____

_____

Correct Answers

A–838

v.—crush

King George III incorrectly thought that it would be easy to **quash** the revolution in America.

A–839

a.—rash

Military leaders who make **impetuous** decisions run the risk of losing battles.

A–840

n.—combatant

The United States did not become a **belligerent** in the First World War until 1917.

Questions

Q–841

ARMISTICE
[`ɑrməstɪs] : 休戰協議

Your Answer

Q–842

CARNAGE
[`kɑrnɪdʒ] : 屠殺

Your Answer

Q–843

SCUTTLE
[`skʌtl̩] : 弄沉

Your Answer

Correct Answers

A–841

n.—truce

On the eleventh day of November 1918, an **armistice** ended World War I.

A–842

n.—slaughter

The **carnage** of the First World War changed the way we look at conflict between nations.

A–843

v.—sink

At the end of the First World War, the Imperial German Navy **scuttled** all its ships so that the Allies would not get them.

Questions

Q–844

BLUFF
[blʌf] : 虛張聲勢

Your Answer _____

Q–845

CONVOY
[ˋkɑnvɔɪ] : 護衛艦

Your Answer _____

Q–846

SCATHING
[ˋskeðɪŋ] : 嚴苛的

Your Answer _____

Correct Answers

A–844

v.—deceive

At the beginning of his rule, Hitler had a weak army, but he gained victories by **bluffing** other countries.

A–845

n.—fleet

During the Second World War, American supply ships sailing for England would travel in large **convoys**.

A–846

a.—harsh

Winston Churchill made many **scathing** remarks about Adolf Hitler.

Questions

Q–847

DISARM
[dɪs`ɑrm] : 解除武裝

Your Answer _____

Q–848

DEFECTION
[dɪ`fɛkʃən]: 脱黨

Your Answer _____

Q–849

INVOKE
[ɪn`vok] : 訴諸於

Your Answer _____

Correct Answers

A–847

v.—give up weapons
At the end of the Second World War, Germany and
Japan **disarmed**.

A–848

n.—desertion
The **defection** of scientists and artists from the Soviet
Union usually received much attention from the news
media in the democracies.

A–849

v.—appeal to
People used to **invoke** a "spirit of history" to explain
historical events.

Questions

Q–850

REGIMENT
[ˋrɛdʒəmənt] : 軍團

Your Answer _____

Q–851

GAUGE
[gedʒ] : 規格

Your Answer _____

Q–852

CHRONICLE
[ˋkranɪkl̩] : 記錄

Your Answer _____

Correct Answers

A–850

n.—group of soldiers

In the British Army, soldiers are very proud of the history of the **regiment** to which they belong.

A–851

n.—size

The Russians use a different **gauge** of railroad track from that of the western Europeans.

A–852

n.—record

In the nineteenth century, it was popular to consider history as being a **chronicle** of the great deeds of great men.

Questions

Q–853

EMPIRICAL
[ɛm`pɪrɪkḷ] : 經驗上的

Your Answer _____

Q–854

ALLEGIANCE
[ə`lidʒəns] : 忠實於

Your Answer _____

Q–855

LEVY
[`lɛvɪ]: 召集，徵用

Your Answer _____

Correct Answers

A–853

a.—experiential, based on data

In the twentieth century, many scholars tried to make history a kind of **empirical** science.

A–854

n.—loyalty

A few thinkers maintain that **allegiance** to all mankind is more important than **allegiance** to the country of one's birth.

A–855

v.—summon by authority

A sovereign state has the right to **levy** troops, and sometimes they use these troops for UN peacekeeping missions.

Questions

Q–856

CONVENE
[kən`vin] : 集合，集會

Your Answer _____

Q–857

EXPLOIT
[ɪk`splɔɪt] [`ɛksplɔɪt] : 利用，剝削

Your Answer _____

Q–858

TENTATIVE
[`tɛntətɪv] : 暫時性的

Your Answer _____

Correct Answers

A–856

v.—come together

Every year, the UN's general assembly **convenes** in New York.

A–857

v.—take advantage of

Some companies **exploit** workers who are in the country illegally.

A–858

a.—temporary

Israelis and Palestinians have reached **tentative** peace agreements many times.

Questions

Q–859

FLOUT
[flaʊt] : 蔑視

Your Answer _____

Q–860

PLOD
[plɑd] : 緩步前進

Your Answer _____

Q–861

CANTER
[ˋkæntɚ] : 快步

Your Answer _____

Correct Answers

A–859

v.—disregard
Some nations **flout** international law.

A–860

v.—move slowly
During a depression, the economy **plods** along.

A–861

n.—an easy gallop
In a recovery, the economy starts moving at a brisk
canter.

Questions

Q–862

REHABILITATE
[ˌrihəˈbɪləˌtet] : 使恢復

Your Answer _____

Q–863

HAMLET
[ˈhæmlɪt] : 小村莊

Your Answer _____

Q–864

BARRICADE
[ˈbærəˌked] : 以屏障阻絕

Your Answer _____

Correct Answers

A–862

v.—restore

Occasionally it happens that a Communist government condemns one of its officials only to **rehabilitate** his reputation years later.

A–863

n.—small village

Huge numbers of people live in cities nowadays, but in centuries past, most people lived on farms or in small **hamlets**.

A–864

v.—block

In today's world, people can no longer **barricade** themselves off from the rest of humanity.

Questions

Q–865

FRACTIOUS
[`frækʃəs] : 好爭論的

Your Answer _____

Q–866

ENVOY
[`ɛnvɔɪ] : 使者，使節

Your Answer _____

Q–867

INEPT
[ɪn`ɛpt] : 笨拙的

Your Answer _____

Correct Answers

A–865

a.—argumentative

Some people accuse the United Nations of being a **fractious** group that can agree on little.

A–866

n.—diplomatic agent

The UN sends **envoys** to deal with problems in especially troubled areas of the world.

A–867

a.—clumsy

The Soviet leaders who tried unsuccessfully to overthrow Mikhail Gorbachev were accused of being **inept** plotters.

Questions

Q–868

PROXY
[ˋprɑksɪ] : 替代的

Your Answer _____

Q–869

DINGY
[ˋdɪndʒɪ] : 黑暗的

Your Answer _____

Q–870

PSYCHE
[ˋsaɪkɪ] : 心靈

Your Answer _____

Correct Answers

A–868

a.—alternate

Although the U.S. and the U.S.S.R. never fought each other directly, they fought a number of small **proxy** wars in the developing world.

A–869

a.—dim, gloomy

Two hundred years ago, mental hospitals were little more than **dingy** prisons.

A–870

n.—mind

Scholars have scientifically studied the human **psyche** for about a century and a half now.

Questions

Q–871

SUBCONSCIOUS
[ˌsəbˋkɑnʃəs] : 潛意識的

Your Answer _____

Q–872

RECOLLECTION
[ˌrɛkəˋlɛkʃən] : 回憶

Your Answer _____

Q–873

AVID
[ˋævɪd] : 熱衷的

Your Answer _____

Correct Answers

A–871

a.—below awareness
Sigmund Freud's theories claim that we all have a **subconscious** mind.

A–872

n.—recall
Freud believed that the **recollection** of childhood problems could help people overcome the problems they have in adulthood.

A–873

a.—enthusiastic
Freud was an **avid** collector of ancient Egyptian, Roman, and Greek art.

Questions

Q–874

ARDUOUS
[`ɑrdʒʊəs] : 需很費心力的

Your Answer _____

Q–875

AFFLICT
[ə`flɪkt] : 受折磨

Your Answer _____

Q–876

DECREPIT
[dɪ`krɛpɪt] : 衰老的

Your Answer _____

Correct Answers

A–874

a.—demanding
For Freud, psychoanalysis was an **arduous** labor that could take years to complete.

A–875

v.—torture
Freudian psychoanalysis does not help people who are **afflicted** with serious disorders like schizophrenia.

A–876

a.—feeble, weak
When Freud was a **decrepit** old man suffering from cancer, he moved to England to escape the Nazis.

Questions

Q–877

RANCOR
[`ræŋkɚ] : 憎恨

Your Answer _____

Q–878

RIGOR
[`rɪgɚ] : 嚴謹

Your Answer _____

Q–879

FACILE
[`fæsl̩] : 簡易的

Your Answer _____

Correct Answers

A–877

n.—bitterness

Early psychologists, who very often had different theories, argued against each other with great **rancor**.

A–878

n.—strictness

Very often with a psychological theory, the more **rigor** it has, the less it explains.

A–879

a.—easy

A therapist should not give a **facile** response to a patient with a serious question.

Questions

Q–880

ARCHAIC
[ɑrˋkeɪk] : 原始的

Your Answer _____

Q–881

FLEETING
[ˋflitɪŋ] : 飛逝的

Your Answer _____

Q–882

HILARIOUS
[həˋlɛrɪəs] : 有趣好笑的

Your Answer _____

Correct Answers

A–880

a.—primitive
Some psychologists believe that modern man still has
a very **archaic** mind.

A–881

a.—swift, passing quickly
The golden age of radio was **fleeting**, but it is still
remembered.

A–882

a.—funny
Some of the old comedy shows on the radio were
quite **hilarious**.

Questions

Q–883

LACHRYMOSE
[ˋlækrəˌmos] : 易流淚的

Your Answer —————————————————

Q–884

EXTEMPORANEOUS
[ɛkˌstɛmpəˋrenɪs] : 未作預演的

Your Answer —————————————————

Q–885

HOAX
[hoks] : 玩笑，惡作劇

Your Answer —————————————————

Correct Answers

A–883

a.—tearful

Listeners would become **lachrymose** as they heard a new episode of their favorite soap opera.

A–884

a.—unrehearsed

Many famous radio shows were either **extemporaneous** performances or live readings of dramatic works.

A–885

n.—trick

Orson Welles broadcast a radio drama about an invasion from Mars, and many think he scared people on purpose by pulling a **hoax**.

Questions

Q–886

BLEEP
[blip] : 發出嗶嗶聲（來消音）

Your Answer _____

Q–887

MYRIAD
[`mɪrɪəd] : 無數，大量

Your Answer _____

Q–888

DECLINE
[dɪ`klaɪn] : 衰落

Your Answer _____

Correct Answers

A–886

v.—beep

Nowadays, radio stations have a four-second delay in live shows so that they can **bleep** out an inappropriate utterance.

A–887

n.—great number

A **myriad** of old radio shows can now be purchased over the World Wide Web.

A–888

n.—fall

The **decline** of radio was brought about by television.

Questions

Q–889

ABANDON
[ə`bændən] : 捨棄

Your Answer _____

_____

Q–890

BETOKEN
[bɪ`tokən] : 預示

Your Answer _____

_____

Q–891

AMPLITUDE
[`æmpləˌtjud] : 幅度

Your Answer _____

_____

Correct Answers

A–889

v.—leave behind
Radio was not **abandoned** when television was invented.

A–890

v.—indicate
We do not know what the coming of satellite radio **betokens** for the world of broadcast media.

A–891

n.—size
AM radio receivers detect changes in **amplitude** in the radio waves at a given frequency.

Questions

Q–892

MODULATE
[ˋmɑdʒəˌlet] : 調整

Your Answer _____

Q–893

MINUSCULE
[ˋmɪnəˌskjul] : 極小的

Your Answer _____

Q–894

SUCCESSOR
[səkˋsɛsə] : 接繼者

Your Answer _____

Correct Answers

A–892

v.—adjust

When one **modulates** the frequency of a radio signal, one is dealing with FM radio.

A–893

a.—tiny

Today's radios' integrated circuitry is of **minuscule** size compared to the ones with vacuum tubes that people bought seventy years ago.

A–894

n.—heir

Television was the **successor** to radio as the most influential and widespread form of communication.

Questions

Q–895

SEMBLANCE
[ˋsɛmbləns] : 外觀，外表

Your Answer _____

_____

Q–896

EDIFY
[ˋɛdəˌfaɪ] : 教化

Your Answer _____

_____

Q–897

LUMINARY
[ˋlumənɛrɪ] : 明星，名人

Your Answer _____

_____

Correct Answers

A–895

n.—appearance
Some television shows have the **semblance** of live broadcasts although they were recorded in advance of being aired.

A–896

v.—educate
The inventor of television thought that it would be used to **edify**, but people wound up using the TV for entertainment.

A–897

n.—celebrity
Some radio **luminaries** successfully made the transition to television.

Questions

Q–898

ENNUI
[ˋɑnwi] : 厭倦

Your Answer _____

Q–899

REVILE
[rɪˋvaɪl] : 瞧不起，輕視

Your Answer _____

Q–900

INNOCUOUS
[ɪˋnɑkjʊəs] : 有害的

Your Answer _____

Correct Answers

A–898

n.—boredom
Some people get a tired feeling of **ennui** after
watching too much television.

A–899

v.—despise
Eventually the inventor of television came to **revile**
his own creation.

A–900

a.—harmless
Some people think that children's cartoons are
innocuous entertainment, but others feel that they
have too much violence in them.

Questions

Q–901

CONJURE
[ˋkʌndʒə] : 變戲法

Your Answer _____

_____

Q–902

HINDER
[ˋhɪndə] : 干擾，阻礙

Your Answer _____

_____

Q–903

PRECLUDE
[prɪˋklud] : 妨礙

Your Answer _____

_____

Correct Answers

A–901

v.—perform magic tricks
Special effects make it easier for a magician to
conjure on television.

A–902

v.—harm
Watching too much TV can **hinder** the development
of good study habits.

A–903

v.—prevent
Sometimes, excessive watching of television
precludes effective studying.

Questions

Q–904

AUSPICE

[`ɔspɪs] : 贊助

Your Answer _____

Q–905

DECEPTIVE

[dɪ`sɛptɪv] : 欺騙的

Your Answer _____

Q–906

INEVITABLE

[ɪn`ɛvətəbl] : 不可避免的

Your Answer _____

Correct Answers

A–904

n.—support

Many good educational programs are made under the **auspices** of public television.

A–905

a.—misleading

Companies that use **deceptive** advertising can run into legal trouble.

A–906

a.—unavoidable

A person who believes that the invention of writing was **inevitable** can draw support from the fact that more than one culture invented a form of writing.

Questions

Q–907

IGNITE
[ɪgˋnaɪt] : 點燃

Your Answer _____

Q–908

TRANSPIRE
[trænˋspaɪr] : 發生

Your Answer _____

Q–909

INSCRIBE
[ɪnˋskraɪb] : 寫，雕在

Your Answer _____

Correct Answers

A–907

v.—kindle

Some thinkers believe that the invention of writing **ignited** the fire of civilization.

A–908

v.—happen

Without written records, it is virtually impossible to learn what **transpired** in ancient times.

A–909

v.—write, mark

The earliest known written characters were **inscribed** on clay tablets.

Questions

Q–910

MUDDLE
[`mʌdḷ] : 亂成一團

Your Answer

Q–911

UNEARTH
[ʌn`ɝθ] : 發掘

Your Answer

Q–912

CUMBROUS
[`kʌmbrəs] : 麻煩的

Your Answer

Correct Answers

A–910

v.—disorganize

In the Middle East, whole libraries of clay tablets
have been dug up, hopelessly **muddled** in their order,
but still in good condition.

A–911

v.—uncover

Archeologists still occasionally **unearth** more clay
tablets.

A–912

a.—troublesome

Some people think that writing systems like the
Chinese and the Egyptian are beautiful to look at, but
they are **cumbrous** and hard to learn since they have
so many symbols.

Questions

Q–913

INTRINSIC
[ɪn`trɪnsɪk] : **本質的**

Your Answer _____

_____

Q–914

ENGENDER
[ɪn`dʒɛndɚ] : **使產生**

Your Answer _____

_____

Q–915

CRYPTIC
[`krɪptɪk] : **神秘的**

Your Answer _____

_____

Correct Answers

A–913

a.—inherent

Some written symbols have an **intrinsic** meaning, like using a single line to represent the number one.

A–914

v.—produce

Slowly but surely, the invention of writing **engendered** huge changes in human consciousness and society.

A–915

a.—mysterious

Ancient Egyptian writing was a **cryptic** puzzle that took centuries to solve.

Questions

Q–916

INVERT
[ɪn`vɜt] : 顛倒過來

Your Answer _____

Q–917

PREMISE
[`prɛmɪs] : 前提

Your Answer _____

Q–918

INDUSTRIOUS
[ɪn`dʌstrɪəs] : 勤勉的

Your Answer _____

Correct Answers

A–916

v.—turn upside down
The capital letter *A* originally looked like a capital *V*
with an added bar, but it was later **inverted**.

A–917

n.—basis
Having a limited set of symbols to represent the
sounds of a language is the **premise** underlying
alphabetic writing.

A–918

a.—diligent
It takes **industrious** practice to develop good
handwriting.

Questions

Q–919

ILLEGIBLE
[ɪˋlɛdʒəbḷ] : 難以辨識的

Your Answer _____

_____

Q–920

IMBUE
[ɪmˋbju] : 使充滿

Your Answer _____

_____

Q–921

AFFINITY
[əˋfɪnətɪ] : 喜愛

Your Answer _____

_____

Correct Answers

A–919

a.—unreadable

People say that physicians have **illegible** handwriting since they had to write a huge number of notes very quickly in medical school.

A–920

v.—fill with

Before printed books became widely available, writing was **imbued** with an almost magical quality.

A–921

n.—attraction

Some people seem to have a natural **affinity** for reading and writing.

Questions

Q–922

CLUTCH
[klʌtʃ] : 緊握

Your Answer _____

Q–923

PAPYRUS
[pə`paɪrəs] : 草紙

Your Answer _____

Q–924

OBLITERATE
[ə`blɪtəˌret] : 除去，毀滅

Your Answer _____

Correct Answers

A–922

v.—grasp
The writer who **clutches** his pen too hard might develop pain in his hand.

A–923

n.—paper made from the papyrus plant
All the books in the famous library at Alexandria, Egypt, were written on scrolls of **papyrus**.

A–924

v.—destroy
Now, with many computers in the world, there could be some electronic books that are impossible to **obliterate** completely.

Questions

Q–925

HINGE
[hɪndʒ] : 決定於

Your Answer _____

Q–926

CAPITALIZE
[ˋkæpətḷˌaɪz] : 利用

Your Answer _____

Q–927

LURK
[lɝk] : 潛藏

Your Answer _____

Correct Answers

A–925

v.—depend

More and more, prosperity **hinges** upon education.

A–926

v.—take advantage

Universities encourage students to **capitalize** on various resources provided for their education and well-being.

A–927

v.—hide

A lot of important information **lurks** inside your college bulletin, so you should read it.

Questions

Q–928

CREDENTIAL
[krɪˋdɛnʃəl] : 證件

Your Answer _____

_____

Q–929

INTEGRATE
[ˋɪntəˏgret] : 綜合，使完整

Your Answer _____

_____

Q–930

HEPATITIS
[ˏhɛpəˋtaɪtɪs] : 肝炎

Your Answer _____

_____

Correct Answers

A–928

n.—certificate

International students usually need to have their **credentials** evaluated or translated into English when applying for school in the U.S.

A–929

v.—combine

International students must work to **integrate** their listening, reading, speaking, and writing skills in English.

A–930

n.—infectious liver disease

Because of state laws, some schools must ask their students to submit proof of immunization against **hepatitis** B.

Questions

Q–931

COMPLY
[kəm`plaɪ] : 依照（規定）

Your Answer _____

Q–932

WAIVE
[wev] : 免除

Your Answer _____

Q–933

PREMIUM
[`primɪəm] : 費用

Your Answer _____

Correct Answers

A–931

v.—abide by, follow
Students who fail to **comply** with vaccination requirements will not be allowed to register for classes.

A–932

v.—remove
Full-time college students are often required to enroll in the school's insurance plan, but the requirement can be **waived** if students have their own insurance plans.

A–933

n.—payment
An insurance **premium** is usually paid along with tuition as students register.

Questions

Q–934

BESET
[bɪˋsɛt] : 使困擾

Your Answer _____

_____

Q–935

LEASE
[lis] : 租借

Your Answer _____

_____

Q–936

APT
[æpt] : 傾向於

Your Answer _____

_____

Correct Answers

A–934

v.—trouble

Shortages of student housing **beset** many urban universities.

A–935

v.—rent

Freshmen tend to live in dormitories, but many older students like to **lease** apartments near campus.

A–936

a.—prone

Some international students are **apt** to become homesick when they first come to America.

Questions

Q–937

MENTOR
[ˋmɛntɚ] : 諮詢者，顧問

Your Answer _____

_____

Q–938

NICHE
[nɪtʃ] [niʃ] : 傾好所在

Your Answer _____

_____

Q–939

SOJOURN
[ˋsodʒɚn] : 渡假

Your Answer _____

_____

Correct Answers

A–937

n.—adviser
Some universities provide a **mentor** to each freshman.

A–938

n.—favorite spot
Some students begin college with a good sense of their own interests, while others might need a few semesters to find their **niche**.

A–939

v.—travel
Students who have money and free time often like to **sojourn** in a warm climate during spring break.

Questions

Q–940

TOURNAMENT
[`tʊrnəmənt] [`tɜnəmənt] : **比賽，錦標賽**

Your Answer _____

_____

Q–941

VIE
[vaɪ] : **競爭**

Your Answer _____

_____

Q–942

HEAVE
[hiv] : **投擲**

Your Answer _____

_____

Correct Answers

A–940

n.—competition
In spring, the college basketball championship is probably the most watched sporting event among fans, and the **tournament** is broadcast on TV nationwide.

A–941

v.—compete
Teams across the United States **vie** for the championship.

A–942

v.—throw
It takes a lot of strength to **heave** a discus far.

Questions

Q–943

SUBLIMATE
[ˋsʌbləˏmet] : 轉移提升

Your Answer _____

_____

Q–944

TRANSCEND
[trænˋsɛnd] : 超越

Your Answer _____

_____

Q–945

EXERTION
[ɪgˋzɝˋʃən] : 努力；用力氣，費心思

Your Answer _____

_____

Correct Answers

A–943

v.—transform

Some athletes **sublimate** their aggressive feelings into good performance on the playing field.

A–944

v.—exceed

The best athlete **transcends** the need to beat others and competes against himself.

A–945

n.—labor

Golf is considered to be good for older people since it requires less **exertion** than many other sports.

Questions

Q–946

EXTRICATE
[`ɛkstrɪ͵ket] : 解救

Your Answer _____

Q–947

EXPEDIENT
[ɪk`spidɪənt] : 方便的，權宜的

Your Answer _____

Q–948

FRENZIED
[`frɛnzɪd] : 狂亂的

Your Answer _____

Correct Answers

A–946

v.—rescue, remove

It can be difficult for a golfer to **extricate** his ball from a sand trap.

A–947

a.—convenient

Good lighting made it **expedient** to have baseball games at night.

A–948

a.—frantic

Some sports fans become **frenzied** while watching their favorite team play.

Questions

Q–949

HUBBUB
[`hʌbʌb] : 吶喊喧囂

Your Answer _____

_____

Q–950

INDEFATIGABLE
[ˌɪndɪ`fætɪgəbl̩] : 不疲倦的，不屈不撓的

Your Answer _____

_____

Q–951

MEDIOCRE
[`midˌɪokə] : 普通的，平凡的

Your Answer _____

_____

Correct Answers

A–949

n.—noise

Cheering fans can cause quite a **hubbub** even before the game begins.

A–950

a.—tireless, untiring

Few people are **indefatigable** enough to run a marathon.

A–951

a.—average, ordinary

With dedication, even a **mediocre** athlete can make a contribution to the team.

Questions

Q–952

PLACID
[`plæsɪd] : 平靜的

Your Answer _____

_____

Q–953

VEXING
[`vɛksɪŋ] : 困擾的

Your Answer _____

_____

Q–954

EXCITABLE
[ɪk`saɪtəb!] : 易情緒激動的

Your Answer _____

_____

Correct Answers

A–952

a.—peaceful

Few things are more relaxing than skating over the smooth surface of a frozen lake on a **placid** winter day.

A–953

a.—annoying

Keeping a neat desk is a **vexing** problem for some students.

A–954

a.—emotional

Excitable students should avoid getting into arguments.

Questions

Q–955

IMPETUS
[`ɪmpətəs] : 激勵

Your Answer

Q–956

FRET
[frɛt] : 擔憂

Your Answer

Q–957

MISHAP
[`mɪsˌhæp] : 不幸的事

Your Answer

Correct Answers

A–955

n.—push, urge, incentive
Sometimes, an upcoming exam provides the **impetus** for a student to study extra hard.

A–956

v.—worry
Students often **fret** about how much they have to study during final exams.

A–957

n.—misfortune
If a class does not go well, you should remember that you can always learn from **mishaps**.

Questions

Q–958

EXPENDITURE
[ɪk`spɛndɪtʃə] : 開銷，花費

Your Answer _____

_____

Q–959

REIMBURSE
[ˌriɪm`bɜs] : 付還，退款

Your Answer _____

_____

Q–960

STIPEND
[`staɪpɛnd] : 助學金，薪水

Your Answer _____

_____

Correct Answers

A–958

n.—expense

International students must watch their **expenditures** since they cannot get jobs off campus.

A–959

v.—repay

If you spend money for your employer, make sure to get **reimbursed**.

A–960

n.—payment, salary

Very often, graduate students receive a **stipend**.

Questions

Q–961

ACCRUE
[əˋkru] : 累積

Your Answer _____

Q–962

REGISTRAR
[ˋrɛdʒɪˌstrɑr] : 在學記錄負責人，註冊組長

Your Answer _____

Q–963

PRUDENT
[ˋprudn̩t] : 明智的

Your Answer _____

Correct Answers

A–961

v.—accumulate

If you pay tuition or fees late, penalties can **accrue**.

A–962

n.—keeper of student records at a university or college

If you want to mail your transcript out, you should go to the **registrar**'s office.

A–963

a.—wise

It is **prudent** to make sure you are registered for the right courses.

Questions

Q–964

CAPACIOUS
[kə`peʃəs] : 寬敞的

Your Answer

Q–965

NOOK
[nʊk]: 角落

Your Answer

Q–966

RECITATION
[ˌrɛsə`teʃən] : 實習課程，補充課程

Your Answer

Correct Answers

A–964

a.—large

It is hard to find a **capacious** room in the library to do a group discussion.

A–965

n.—corner

If you can, find a quiet **nook** in the library or your dormitory where you can study free from distractions.

A–966

n.—work group for a course

It is common for some undergraduate courses to have a **recitation** scheduled as part of the course.

Questions

Q–967

IMMERSE
[ɪˋmɝs] : 完全投入

Your Answer

Q–968

PANTOMIME
[ˋpæntəˌmaɪm] : 動作，手勢

Your Answer

Q–969

ARCHIVE
[ˋɑrkaɪv] : 檔案

Your Answer

Correct Answers

A–967

v.—plunge

Some people believe that you will learn a foreign language faster if you **immerse** yourself in an environment where it is spoken all the time.

A–968

n.—communicating by gesturing without talking

Some foreign language teachers use **pantomime** to convey the meaning of a new word.

A–969

n.—record

Many newspapers and journals make their **archives** available on line.

Questions

Q–970

DISPOSAL
[dɪˋspozḷ] : 掌握；使用權

Your Answer _____

_____

Q–971

AFFLUENCE
[ˋæflʊəns] : 富足

Your Answer _____

_____

Q–972

LIAISON
[ˋlieˏzɑn] : 連絡人

Your Answer _____

_____

Correct Answers

A–970

n.—control

One of the librarian's jobs is to put information at your **disposal**, so don't be afraid to ask questions.

A–971

n.—wealth, plenty

The **affluence** of libraries and museums is of a cultural nature although their collections can have a great monetary value.

A–972

n.—contact

A library **liaison** is familiar with the library's collections and resources.

Questions

Q–973

GLEAN
[glin] : 蒐集

Your Answer _____

_____

Q–974

IMPART
[ɪm`part] : 給予

Your Answer _____

_____

Q–975

AFFILIATE
[ə`fɪlɪˌet] : 附屬於

Your Answer _____

_____

Correct Answers

A–973

v.—gather

Sometimes, a student writing a history paper will try to **glean** important facts from old newspapers.

A–974

v.—give

Librarians **impart** research skills to those who ask for help.

A–975

v.—associate

Students can use libraries that are **affiliated** with their school.

Questions

Q–976

COMPENDIUM
[kəm`pɛndɪəm] : 概略

Your Answer _____

Q–977

CONTENTION
[kən`tɛnʃən] : 爭議

Your Answer _____

Q–978

SUNDRY
[`sʌndrɪ] : 各式各樣的

Your Answer _____

Correct Answers

A–976

n.—short manual or guide
Very often, it is handy to have a **compendium** of
English grammar by your side when you are writing
a paper.

A–977

n.—argument
Some points of style and grammar can be sources of
contention among different professors.

A–978

a.—various
Most professors are going to grade you on the basis
of the quality of your ideas and the clarity of your
thinking rather than on **sundry** points of grammar.

Questions

Q–979

SYLLABUS
['sɪləbəs] : 課程綱要，課程大綱

Your Answer _____

_____

Q–980

SYNOPSIS
[sɪ`nɑpsɪs] : 摘要，大意

Your Answer _____

_____

Q–981

GIST
[dʒɪst] : 要旨，大意

Your Answer _____

_____

Correct Answers

A–979

n.—course description

On the first day of class, your professor should give you a **syllabus** that clearly lists what you are required to do in the course.

A–980

n.—summary

If you are writing a long research paper, it is a good idea to put a brief **synopsis** at the beginning that mentions what you are going to discuss.

A–981

n.—main point

Try to get the **gist** of a research paper before you decide whether to use it in your own term paper.

Questions

Q–982

DISSECT
[dɪ`sɛkt] [daɪ`sɛkt]: 分析

Your Answer _____

Q–983

SPECIFICATION
[ˌspɛsəfə`keʃən] : 規定

Your Answer _____

Q–984

AMORPHOUS
[ə`mɔrfəs] : 無組織的

Your Answer _____

Correct Answers

A–982

v.—analyze, examine

If a theory seems complicated, you need to **dissect** it into smaller concepts that are easier to grasp.

A–983

n.—guideline, requirement

Students who understand and meet the **specifications** set by their professors have an advantage over those who don't.

A–984

a.—formless, disorganized

Writing is an exacting process that takes you from a few **amorphous** ideas to a carefully reasoned finished product.

Questions

Q–985

PARAMOUNT
[`pærə‚maʊnt] : 主要的

Your Answer _____

Q–986

QUANDARY
[`kwɑndərɪ] : 困境

Your Answer _____

Q–987

ENUMERATE
[ɪ`njumə‚ret] : 列舉

Your Answer _____

Correct Answers

A–985

a.—chief

Logically organizing your thoughts is of **paramount** importance when writing a paper.

A–986

n.—dilemma

You should consult with your professor if you are in a **quandary** about what to write.

A–987

v.—specify

You need to **enumerate** your points in a way that the reader can follow easily.

Questions

Q–988

TANGENT
[`tændʒənt] : 離題

Your Answer _____

_____

Q–989

VEER
[vɪr] : 改變方向

Your Answer _____

_____

Q–990

PARENTHESIS
[pə`rɛnθəsɪs] : 括弧

Your Answer _____

_____

Correct Answers

A-988

n.—digression

When you write a paper, it is important to keep to your main point and not go off on a **tangent**.

A-989

v.—turn

You need to stay focused and not **veer** from your topic.

A-990

n.—a pair of signs that mark off a side comment (like this)

If you need to enclose an extra comment, you can use **parentheses**.

Questions

Q–991

FOOTNOTE
[`fʊt͵not] : 註腳

Your Answer _____

_____

Q–992

INDENT
[ɪn`dɛnt] : 段首縮排 （起段空格）

Your Answer _____

_____

Q–993

RECAPITULATE
[͵rikə`pɪtʃə͵let] : 重述要點

Your Answer _____

_____

Correct Answers

A-991

n.—note

Extra information that seems independent of the text can be put in a **footnote**.

A-992

v.—begin further in

It makes things easier on the reader if you **indent** the first line of each new paragraph.

A-993

v.—summarize

At the end of a term paper, it is good to have a paragraph that **recapitulates** the main points you have made.

Questions

Q–994

APPEND
[ə`pɛnd] : 附加

Your Answer _____

Q–995

WILLY-NILLY
[`wɪlɪ`nɪlɪ] : 未經準備地

Your Answer _____

Q–996

OVERSIGHT
[`ovɚˌsaɪt] : 粗心大意

Your Answer _____

Correct Answers

A–994

v.—attach

You can **append** notes to the end of each page or at the end of your paper.

A–995

adv.—without a plan

You need to think in advance about the structure of your paper and avoid writing **willy-nilly** at the last moment.

A–996

n.—neglect

Even when you use a spell checker, **oversight** and lack of careful checking can leave errors in your writing.

Questions

Q–997

PROOFREAD
[`prufˌrid] : 校對

Your Answer _____

_____

Q–998

PROCLIVITY
[pro`klıvətı] : 傾向

Your Answer _____

_____

Q–999

CONTINGENT
[kən`tındʒənt] : 視（某情況）而定的

Your Answer _____

_____

Correct Answers

A–997

v.—double-check

Make sure that you **proofread** your paper before you submit it to your professor.

A–998

n.—tendency

Some students have a **proclivity** for submitting their work late.

A–999

a.—dependent

Very often, your class grade can be **contingent** on attendance.

Questions

Q–1000

PRAGMATIC

[præg`mætɪk] : 實用的

Your Answer _____

_____

Q–1001

PRELUDE

[`prɛljud] : 序幕

Your Answer _____

_____

Q–1002

QUINTESSENTIAL

[ˌkwɪntə`sɛnʃəl] : 精髓的，典型的

Your Answer _____

_____

Correct Answers

A–1000

a.—practical

Most students could use some **pragmatic** advice about writing a term paper.

A–1001

n.—introduction

"Pomp and Circumstance" is a musical piece that serves as a **prelude** to many graduation ceremonies.

A–1002

a.—ideal

A **quintessential** part of every graduation ceremony is a speech by a famous or accomplished person.

Questions

Q–1003

BESTOW
[bɪˋsto] : 授予

Your Answer _____

_____

Q–1004

COMMENCEMENT
[kəˋmɛnsmənt] : 畢業典禮

Your Answer _____

_____

Correct Answers

Index

A

abandon, 593
abate, 347
abortive, 237
abrasive, 327
abrogate, 525
absolve, 393
absorb, 299
abstain, 403
abstemious, 239
abundantly, 299
abyss, 297
accelerate, 317
accessibility, 57
accommodate, 377
accomplice, 395
accost, 131
accountability, 435
accrue, 641
accumulate, 383
acoustic, 337
acquire, 481
acquit, 393
acrid, 487
acronym, 359
acumen, 111
adamant, 65
adequate, 485
adhere, 403
adhesiveness, 139
administer, 495
adulterate, 197
advent, 319
advocate, 87
aerosol, 281
aesthetic, 15
affable, 413
affiliate, 649
affinity, 613
afflict, 583
affluence, 647
aggravate, 443
aggregate, 509
agility, 461
agitate, 199
agonize, 419
ailment, 183
alacrity, 251
albeit, 509
alienate, 441
alight, 129
align, 263
allegiance, 569

alleviate, 229
allocate, 385
allot, 377
allusion, 107
aloof, 105
amend, 209
amenity, 97
amnesia, 167
amorphous, 655
amphibian, 147
amplitude, 593
anachronism, 471
animated, 359
animosity, 355
annex, 417
annihilate, 353
annotate, 35
anomalous, 141
anomaly, 253
anticipate, 73
antiquity, 541
antiseptic, 181
apathetic, 445
appall, 511
apparatus, 361
apparel, 523
appeal, 77
append, 663
appraisal, 7
apprehensive, 379
appropriate, 493
apt, 623
aquatic, 301
aqueous, 297
arbiter, 543
arbitrary, 1
archaeology, 449
archaic, 587
archive, 645
ardent, 103
ardor, 465
arduous, 583
arid, 311
aristocrat, 379
armistice, 561
array, 483
artifact, 451
ascertain, 321
ascribe, 71
aseptic, 191
aspire, 241
assent, 69
assiduously, 73
assimilate, 55

asteroid, 253
astounding, 451
astute, 515
atmospheric, 321
attenuate, 347
attribute, 543
audacious, 479
augment, 541
auspice, 603
austerity, 389
autocratic, 405
autopsy, 397
avarice, 7
avert, 287
avian, 179
avid, 581
avow, 53
axis, 275
azure, 299

B

badger, 461
balmy, 135
baneful, 279
banter, 415
barren, 313
barricade, 575
bedeck, 465
behold, 267
belie, 249
belligerent, 559
bereaved, 255
beset, 623
bestow, 669
betoken, 593
bibliophile, 473
bigotry, 49
bizarre, 261
blast, 437
bleep, 591
blemish, 163
blight, 127
bluff, 563
bog, 411
bolster, 33
bona fide, 473
brawl, 391
breach, 497
brittle, 453
bucolic, 1
butt, 467

C

cabal, 537
cacophonous, 343
callous, 427
camouflage, 145
candid, 557
candor, 425
canter, 573
capacious, 643
capitalize, 617
capricious, 431
captivate, 527
cardinal, 127
carnage, 561
cascading, 369
celestial, 257
censor, 527
centennial, 89
chameleon, 143
characteristic, 325
chasm, 51
chronicle, 567
chum, 413
circumscribe, 487
circumvent, 225
clamor, 353
clandestine, 479
cling, 137
clog, 215
clutch, 615
clutter, 207
coalesce, 251
cogent, 405
coin, 141
collusion, 503
colossal, 59
colt, 133
commencement, 669
compendium, 651
compensation, 505
compile, 29
complimentary, 33
comply, 621
compress, 331
compulsion, 409
concede, 39
conceivable, 59
concoct, 199
concur, 211
concurrent, 317
condolence, 425
condone, 529

confine, 197
confound, 279
congenial, 255
congenital, 221
congregate, 489
conjecture, 79
conjure, 601
consecutive, 421
consensus, 217
consolidate, 501
consort, 9
conspicuous, 291
conspire, 395
constraint, 69
contagious, 173
contaminated, 183
contemptuous, 551
contention, 651
contentious, 195
contiguous, 507
contingency, 181
contingent, 665
convection, 143
convene, 571
convoy, 563
corpulent, 237
counterfeit, 9
cove, 15
crass, 13
craze, 521
credence, 381
credential, 619
crucial, 71
crusade, 201
cryptic, 609
culmination, 81
culture, 187
cumbersome, 271
cumbrous, 607
curb, 217
cursory, 37
curtail, 55
cynical, 437

D

dauntless, 551
dazzling, 309
dearth, 257
deceptive, 603
deciduous, 115
decline, 591
declivity, 125
decrepit, 583

deduce, 283
default, 537
defection, 565
deference, 555
defiant, 355
defy, 61
degenerate, 367
degradation, 315
dejected, 431
delineate, 379
delude, 497
deluge, 493
demagogue, 387
demise, 373
demote, 263
denote, 83
deplete, 285
deploy, 373
deposition, 399
deprive, 167
desolate, 311
despondent, 429
deteriorate, 315
detest, 231
detrimental, 185
devastating, 177
deviate, 467
devious, 199
devoid, 311
devour, 265
dexterous, 111
dictum, 473
diffusion, 351
dignify, 531
digress, 381
dilate, 157
dilute, 349
diminish, 285
diminutive, 547
dingy, 579
disarm, 565
discernible, 145
discharge, 319
disclosure, 207
disconcert, 495
discrete, 163
discretion, 205
dismal, 155
disparate, 543
disparity, 545
dispatch, 469
dispel, 445
dispersion, 327
displace, 53

disposal, 647
disrupt, 165
dissect, 655
disseminate, 447
dissension, 465
dissonance, 109
distilled, 333
distort, 29
distraught, 457
divergent, 193
diverse, 41
divert, 33
divisibility, 291
divulge, 259
docile, 127
dogmatic, 513
dormant, 261
dumbfound, 93
dungeon, 557
dynamic, 545

E

E. coli, 123
ecclesiastical, 247
edify, 597
efface, 67
effervesce, 241
efficacy, 227
elapse, 321
elation, 429
elicit, 437
eliminate, 347
elongate, 145
elucidate, 5
elude, 531
elusive, 135
emaciated, 239
emanate, 345
emancipate, 407
embellish, 27
embezzle, 397
embitter, 463
emblem, 93
embody, 79
embrace, 243
emergence, 319
eminent, 289
emissary, 257
emission, 283
empirical, 569
emulate, 95
enchant, 305
encompass, 483

encumber, 369
endorse, 443
endowment, 3
energize, 225
engender, 609
engrave, 329
enigma, 363
enlist, 55
ennui, 599
enormously, 297
enrage, 389
enrapture, 107
entail, 527
enthrall, 1
enticing, 223
enumerate, 657
envisage, 447
envision, 273
envoy, 577
equilibrium, 365
equinox, 275
equitable, 401
eradicate, 287
erosion, 315
err, , 443
erratic, 165
erroneous, 547
erudite, 411
eschew, 25
estimable, 137
eulogy, 425
evasion, 539
evoke, 85
excavation, 449
excitable, 635
excruciating, 343
exemplary, 555
exempt, 209
exertion, 629
exhume, 399
expedient, 631
expeditious, 469
expel, 305
expenditure, 639
explicitly, 213
exploit, 571
exponent, 21
expound, 71
expurgate, 39
extant, 133
extemporaneous, 589
extensive, 3
extinct, 541
extol, 481

extort, 49
extraneous, 251
extricate, 631
exude, 413

F

fabricate, 31
facade, 89
facet, 323
facile, 585
fallacious, 419
fallow, 121
famished, 227
fatuous, 265
feasible, 69
fecundity, 129
feign, 499
fermenting, 243
ferocious, 137
fervent, 417
festoon, 101
fickle, 147
fictitious, 463
figment, 5
filthy, 435
flagrant, 203
flamboyant, 77
fleeting, 587
flimsy, 93
flora, 115
flout, 573
fluctuate, 519
fluffy, 293
fluster, 237
flux, 245
foliage, 117
footnote, 661
forcible, 401
forego, 195
forge, 489
fractious, 577
fraud, 497
fraudulent, 31
frayed, 11
frenzied, 631
fret, 637
frigid, 117
frugal, 515
fruition, 411
fulminate, 529
fusion, 375

G

gabbling, 545
gait, 161
gale, 119
gamut, 115
garner, 387
garrulous, 535
gaseous, 277
gash, 157
gaudy, 95
gauge, 567
gazette, 35
gem, 323
genesis, 253
genuine, 25
germinate, 479
ghastly, 247
gist, 653
glaze, 223
glean, 649
glut, 523
graft, 141
gratify, 461
grid, 371
grip, 533
grumble, 5
guise, 383

H

habitat, 303
haggle, 467
hallmark, 83
hamlet, 575
hamper, 235
haphazard, 41
harass, 495
harmonious, 341
harrowing, 291
hatchet, 539
hazardous, 309
hazy, 357
heave, 627
hectic, 41
heinous, 39
hepatitis, 619
heredity, 149
heretic, 249
heyday, 471
hilarious, 587
hinder, 601
hinge, 617
hoax, 589

homogeneous, 119
hubbub, 633
hue, 75
husbandry, 131
hybrid, 119
hydrogenate, 213
hyperbolic, 37
hypothesize, 255

I

icon, 101
ideology, 539
ignite, 605
illegible, 613
illicit, 135
illuminate, 3
imbue, 613
immerse, 645
immobility, 293
impair, 169
impart, 649
impartial, 393
impeach, 421
impeccable, 99
impede, 343
impediment, 245
impermeable, 345
impervious, 19
impetuous, 559
impetus, 637
implement, 211
impregnable, 551
impromptu, 383
impropriety, 385
improvident, 349
improvise, 45
impurity, 293
incapacitate, 157
incarcerate, 555
incentive, 51
incessant, 309
inclination, 439
incongruity, 97
incontrovertible, 289
incorporate, 79
incredulity, 249
incredulous, 63
increment, 351
incumbent, 449
incur, 499
indefatigable, 633
indemnify, 499

indent, 661
indictment, 401
indigenous, 507
indignity, 421
indispensable, 303
indulgent, 169
industrious, 611
inept, 577
inevitable, 603
inflammation, 181
inflict, 289
influenza, 171
infrastructure, 59
ingenious, 63
inhibit, 187
inkling, 221
innate, 377
innocuous, 599
inordinate, 505
insatiable, 475
inscribe, 605
insidiously, 281
insinuate, 385
insomnia, 243
instigate, 457
insulate, 277
integer, 111
integrate, 619
interface, 331
intermittent, 487
intestinal, 187
intractable, 155
intrepid, 363
intricate, 73
intrigue, 339
intrinsic, 609
intrusion, 493
intuitive, 151
inure, 375
invective, 477
inveigh, 123
inverse, 337
invert, 611
invoke, 565
irascible, 123
irate, 9
irksome, 129
irrefutable, 367
irreparable, 21
irrigation, 317
itinerant, 121

J

jangle, 109
jarring, 107
jeopardy, 261
jolt, 235
jumble, 35
jurisdiction, 391

K

kindred, 151
knack, 431

L

labyrinthine, 381
lachrymose, 589
laconic, 471
lash, 491
laud, 535
lavish, 99
leach, 351
lease, 623
lethal, 177
lethargic, 457
leverage, 515
levy, 569
liaison, 647
loafer, 485
loathe, 231
locomotion, 273
longevity, 219
loot, 453
lubricant, 229
lucrative, 455
ludicrous, 77
lug, 481
luminary, 597
lunatic, 267
lurk, 617
luster, 327
lustrous, 11

M

maim, 159
malady, 163
malign, 433
malignant, 161
mandate, 531
mandatory, 205
maneuver, 501
mediocre, 633

membrane, 183
mentor, 625
metabolism, 239
meticulously, 361
mince, 231
minuscule, 595
misgiving, 445
mishap, 637
modulate, 595
monarchy, 553
monumental, 81
morbid, 235
motif, 97
muddle, 607
mundane, 85
murky, 125
mutable, 519
mutate, 179
myriad, 591

N

nausea, 159
negligible, 207
nettle, 525
niche, 625
nocturnal, 11
nook, 643
noted, 339
novice, 125
null, 271

O

oblique, 331
obliterate, 615
obsolete, 23
obviate, 511
offensive, 435
offset, 511
offshoot, 83
omen, 263
ongoing, 195
onset, 155
opaque, 17
opulence, 553
oscillate, 335
outlying, 43
outpost, 275
outspoken, 503
overhaul, 517
oversee, 209
oversight, 663

Index

P

palatable, 215
panacea, 475
pandemic, 177
pantomime, 645
papyrus, 615
paradigm, 219
paradoxical, 165
parameter, 57
paramount, 657
parenthesis, 659
pasteurize, 189
pathogenic, 191
pecuniary, 505
pedestal, 91
pejorative, 37
pendulum, 335
percussion, 341
perjury, 399
perpendicular, 61
perpetrator, 153
perpetual, 365
perplexing, 525
pertain, 91
pertinent, 295
pervasive, 175
pester, 529
petition, 211
petrify, 47
pigment, 17
pillage, 453
pinnacle, 295
pinpoint, 359
placate, 427
placid, 635
plebeian, 427
plod, 573
plunder, 13
plunge, 67
ply, 535
ponderous, 387
postmortem, 397
postulate, 285
practitioner, 233
pragmatic, 667
precarious, 517
precipitation, 313
preclude, 601
precocious, 459
preconception, 513
predatory, 131
predicament, 373
predilection, 223

predisposition, 171
predominant, 171
prelude, 667
premier, 197
premise, 611
premium, 621
presage, 265
preservative, 203
prestige, 29
presumption, 391
prevalent, 175
probe, 269
proclaim, 407
proclivity, 665
procrastinate, 31
prodigious, 301
profane, 549
profuse, 301
prohibit, 205
proliferation, 375
promulgate, 557
proofread, 665
propagate, 333
propensity, 153
proponent, 193
proscribed, 549
protocol, 287
protracted, 549
provision, 491
proximity, 345
proxy, 579
prudent, 641
pseudonym, 101
psyche, 579
pungent, 233
purge, 241
purport, 189

Q

qualm, 45
quandary, 657
quash, 559
quell, 403
quibble, 441
quintessential, 667

R

raconteur, 105
radical, 477
rampant, 455
rancid, 213
rancor, 585

rapture, 269
ratify, 389
raze, 547
rebate, 469
rebuke, 423
rebut, 353
recapitulate, 661
receptive, 355
recitation, 643
recollection, 581
recount, 103
recourse, 51
refract, 329
refrain, 357
refurbish, 87
regiment, 567
registrar, 641
rehabilitate, 575
reimburse, 639
reiterate, 533
relapse, 221
relegate, 259
relentlessly, 65
relinquish, 415
remnant, 109
renounce, 121
renovate, 89
renowned, 339
repel, 433
replenish, 369
repudiate, 95
residue, 349
resilient, 227
resonant, 337
respiratory, 173
retribution, 405
retrograde, 247
retrospect, 423
reverberate, 217
revile, 599
rife, 489
rigor, 585
rudimentary, 225
rustic, 117

S

sabotage, 371
sagacious, 133
sallow, 233
salvage, 91
sanity, 367
sarcasm, 441
satire, 103

saturate, 475
savor, 229
scant, 313
scathing, 563
scintilla, 365
scoff, 419
scourge, 173
scribble, 417
scruple, 47
scrupulous, 451
scrutinize, 281
scrutiny, 27
scuffle, 459
scurry, 519
scuttle, 561
seasoned, 517
secluded, 43
secrete, 19
semblance, 597
sequel, 463
shackle, 25
sibling, 151
simulate, 271
simultaneously, 323
slander, 433
slant, 99
slit, 477
sluggish, 167
smear, 7
smother, 307
smudge, 27
snarl, 53
sojourn, 625
soporific, 169
spate, 521
spearhead, 201
specification, 655
speck, 185
spoilage, 189
spontaneous, 21
sporadic, 485
spree, 513
squall, 361
squander, 533
sterilize, 191
stifle, 307
stipend, 639
stipulate, 407
stout, 341
straightforward, 439
strain, 307
streamline, 81
strife, 507
stringent, 179

strive, 87
stupendous, 501
subconscious, 581
sublimate, 629
subside, 245
subsidize, 67
subsidy, 503
subterranean, 295
successor, 595
succumb, 65
suffice, 509
sundry, 651
superfluous, 113
supersede, 47
surmise, 357
surmount, 61
susceptible, 279
sustainable, 57
sustenance, 305
syllabus, 653
symbiotic, 303
symmetrical, 147
synchronize, 483
synopsis, 653
synthetic, 325

T

tally, 429
tamper, 363
tangent, 659
tangible, 273
tantalize, 159
tantamount, 409
taper, 523
taut, 23
teem, 185
tenaciously, 139
tentative, 571
tenuous, 459
terminology, 113
terrestrial, 149
therapeutic, 143
thermal, 329
tint, 325
tournament, 627
tranquil, 43
transcend, 629
transitory, 113
translucent, 17
transpire, 605
traverse, 49
treacherous, 13
trickle, 23

trustworthy, 409
tumult, 423
tyro, 15

U

ubiquitous, 215
undermine, 219
underpinning, 153
underscore, 553
undulating, 161
unduly, 75
unearth, 607
unequivocal, 439
unprecedented, 63
unravel, 269
unscathed, 415
unsettling, 45
unsolicited, 491
uproar, 259
upsurge, 521

V

vandalism, 371
vanguard, 201
varnish, 19
veer, 659
vehemently, 203
velocity, 333
venerable, 267
verify, 283
vernal, 277
versatile, 139
vertebrate, 149
vexing, 635
vibration, 335
vie, 627
vigilance, 455
vigorous, 193
vindicate, 395
virulent, 175

W

waive, 621
whereby, 537
willy-nilly, 663
withstand, 85
woo, 447
wretched, 75

Z

zenith, 105